quick & easy

cooking
for one

molly perham

foulsham

LONDON • **NEW YORK** • **TORONTO** • **SYDNEY**

foulsham

The Publishing House, Bennetts Close, Cippenham,
Berkshire, SL1 5AP, England

ISBN 0-572-02694-3

Printed in Great Britain by The Bath Press, Bath

Contents

Introduction

Eating alone should be much more fun than cooking a solitary pork chop or heating a packaged ready-made meal in the microwave. With only yourself to please, you can try out exciting new recipes and eat exactly what you want, when you want it. 'All very well,' I hear you say, 'but it's not worth cooking just for me – it takes too much time.' It can do – but then nobody should expect to produce a three-course meal for themselves every night, or any night, come to that!

The recipes in this book are as quick and easy as grilling (broiling) a pork chop. They are all cooked on top of the stove, so you don't even have to turn on the oven. Most are just the right size for one portion, but some recipes make two servings, so that you can eat one immediately and then store the other in the fridge or freezer.

I've also included lots of tips on how you might save time by organising your shopping efficiently.

Shopping and Equipment

Finding time to go food shopping can be almost as difficult as finding time to cook. The key to making it easier is to keep your storecupboard and fridge stocked with the basics, so that you have the necessary ingredients to produce a quick and easy meal for one at any time, day or night.

With a bit of planning, you can do just one basic shop once a week – only milk, bread and fresh meat and poultry need to be bought more often (unless you have a freezer). For the recipes in this book, the following checklist of items will be useful. As you use each item from your storecupboard, remember to make a note to replace it when you do your next basic shop.

Packets and jars

Sugar – brown and caster (superfine)
Honey – clear
Plain (all-purpose) flour
Cornflour (cornstarch)
Pasta – spaghetti, tagliatelli, pasta shapes
Rice – long-grain and round
Medium egg noodles
Quick-cook couscous
Lentils – red and green
Cooking oils – vegetable or sunflower, plus
olive and sesame
Wine vinegar
Lemon juice – in a plastic container or bottle
Soy sauce
Pesto
Chilli sauce
Mustard – Dijon and English
Tomato purée (paste)
Curry powder and paste
Stock cubes – beef, chicken and vegetable
Nuts – flaked (slivered) almonds, pine nuts,
whole cashews and walnuts
Seeds – sunflower and sesame
Dried fruit – apricots and raisins
Olives

Herbs and seasonings

Dried herbs – basil, thyme, oregano and mixed
herbs
Salt
Black peppercorns for grinding
Cayenne
Spices – ground ginger, cinnamon, turmeric,
paprika, cumin and coriander (cilantro), grated
nutmeg and cumin
and coriander seeds
Chilli powder

Cans

Tomatoes
Tuna fish
Salmon
Chick peas (garbanzos)
Red kidney beans
Borlotti and/or cannellini beans
Butter (lima) beans

In the fridge

Butter
Margarine
Eggs
Cheddar cheese
Parmesan cheese
Milk
Cream
Yoghurt
Crème fraîche
Ham
Bacon

In the freezer compartment

Peas
Beans
Sweetcorn (corn)
Spinach

Fresh fruit and vegetables

Lettuce – iceberg keeps particularly well
Tomatoes
Cucumber
Spring onions (scallions)
(Bell) peppers – green, red, yellow
Courgettes (zucchini)
Aubergines (eggplants)
All the above will keep for up to a week in the
fridge.
Fresh herbs – keep in a plastic bag or, even
better, grow them in pots on the windowsill
Potatoes
Onions
Garlic
Fresh root ginger
These last four items should be stored in a cool,
dark cupboard, where they will all keep for up
to a week.

Equipment

Don't worry if your cooking facilities and equipment are limited. The following list contains everything that you will need for preparing and cooking the meals in this book.

Large, non-stick frying pan (skillet)
Saucepans, one large and one small, with lids
Ovenproof (e.g. Pyrex) dishes
Mixing bowls, one large and one small
Measuring jug
Scales
Metal sieve (strainer)
Cheese grater
Can opener
Bottle opener
Slotted spoon
Spatula
Wooden spoon
Sharp knife
Chopping board
Spoons – tablespoon, dessertspoon and teaspoon

Measurements

If you don't own a measuring jug and scales, these rough guides should be useful:
1 ordinary mug holds 300 ml/½ pt/1¼ cups
1 small teacup holds about
120 ml/4 fl oz/½ cup
1 2.5 cm/1 in cube of butter or margarine weighs about 25 g/1 oz
1 handful of pasta shapes weighs about
75 g/3 oz

Notes on the recipes

✳ Do not mix metric, imperial and American measures. Follow one set only.

✳ American terms are given in brackets.

✳ All spoon measurements are level: 1 tsp = 5 ml; 1 tbsp = 15 ml.

✳ Eggs are medium unless otherwise stated.

✳ Always wash, peel, core and seed, if necessary, fresh foods before use. Ensure that all produce is as fresh as possible and in good condition.

✳ Seasoning and the use of strongly flavoured ingredients, such as onions and garlic, are very much a matter of personal taste. Taste the food as you cook and adjust seasoning to suit your own taste.

✳ Always use fresh herbs unless dried are specifically called for. If it is necessary to use dried herbs, use half the quantity stated. Chopped, frozen varieties are much better than dried. There is no substitute for fresh parsley and coriander (cilantro).

✳ Can and packet sizes are approximate and will depend on the particular brand.

✳ Use your own discretion in substituting ingredients and personalising the recipes. Make notes of particular successes as you go along.

Soups and Snacks

Soup is a wonderful solution when you want to make a quick snack for one, and the tasty soups in this section don't take much more effort than opening a can, taste ten times better and cost considerably less. Some of them need to be liquidised, but if you don't have a liquidiser, you could buy a mouli-légumes, which works by hand and is much cheaper. The other option is to push everything through a sieve (strainer).

The amounts given for these soups make two servings. They will all keep for a couple of days in the fridge, but when reheating make sure you bring them to the boil.

I have also included ideas for quick snacks, using French bread, ciabatta, bagels, pittas and muffins – and none of them takes any more time than everyone's favourite standby, cheese on toast.

Courgette Soup

Makes 2 servings
15 ml/1 tbsp olive oil
25 g/1 oz/2 tbsp butter or margarine
450 g/1 lb courgettes (zucchini), sliced
1 small onion, sliced
225 g/8 oz potatoes, quartered
2.5 ml/½ tsp ground cumin
300 ml/½ pt/1¼ cups chicken or vegetable stock
300 ml/½ pt/1¼ cups milk
Salt and freshly ground black pepper
2 sprigs of parsley, to garnish

1   Heat the oil and butter or margarine in a large saucepan. Add the courgettes and onion and cook over a moderate heat for about 5 minutes until just beginning to brown.

2   Add all the remaining ingredients. Bring to the boil, then reduce the heat and simmer for about 15 minutes until the potatoes are soft.

3   Blend in a liquidiser or rub through a sieve (strainer) until smooth.

4   Check and adjust the seasoning, and serve in warm bowls, garnished with sprigs of parsley.

25 minutes to prepare

Carrot and Ginger Soup

Makes 2 servings
25 g/1 oz/2 tbsp butter or margarine
225 g/8 oz carrots, thinly sliced
15 ml/1 tbsp grated fresh root ginger
450 ml/¾ pt/2 cups vegetable stock
Salt and freshly ground black pepper
30 ml/2 tbsp plain yoghurt
2 sprigs of parsley, to garnish

1 Melt half the butter or margarine in a saucepan, add the carrots and ginger and cook gently for 10 minutes.

2 Stir in the stock, bring to the boil, then reduce the heat and cook for about 10 minutes until the carrots are soft.

3 Blend in a liquidiser or rub through a sieve (strainer) until smooth.

4 Return the soup to the saucepan to reheat, stir in the remaining butter or margarine and season to taste with salt and pepper.

5 Serve in warm bowls, garnished with a swirl of yoghurt and a sprig of parsley.

⏱ 25 minutes to prepare

Italian Bean and Pasta Soup

Makes 2 servings

10 ml/2 tsp sunflower or vegetable oil
1 small onion, chopped
1 garlic clove, crushed
1 carrot, finely diced
1 celery stick, chopped
5 ml/1 tsp tomato purée (paste)
600 ml/1 pt/2½ cups beef stock
200 g/7 oz/1 small can of borlotti beans
25 g/1 oz small pasta shapes
25 g/1 oz frozen peas
Salt and freshly ground black pepper

1 Heat the oil in a large saucepan. Add the onion, garlic, carrot and celery and cook gently for 5 minutes.

2 Add the tomato purée, stock and beans. Bring to the boil, then reduce the heat, cover and simmer for 10 minutes.

3 Add the pasta and peas and cook for a further 7 minutes until the pasta is just tender.

4 Season to taste with salt and pepper, then serve in warm bowls.

🕐 25 minutes to prepare

Tomato and Peperami Soup

Makes 2 servings

5 ml/2 tsp sunflower or vegetable oil
1 small onion, chopped
1 garlic clove, crushed
½ small red (bell) pepper, seeded and chopped
200 g/7 oz/1 small can of chopped tomatoes
600 ml/1 pt/2½ cups beef stock
5 ml/1 tsp Worcestershire sauce
Salt and freshly ground black pepper
1 small peperami sausage, chopped
25 g/1 oz small pasta shapes

1 Heat the oil in a large saucepan. Add the onion, garlic and pepper and fry (sauté) gently for 2 minutes.

2 Add the chopped tomatoes, half the beef stock and the Worcestershire sauce. Season with salt and pepper.

3 Bring to the boil, then reduce the heat, cover and simmer for 15 minutes.

4 Blend in a liquidiser or rub through a sieve (strainer) until smooth.

5 Return the blended mixture to the pan and add the remaining stock, the chopped sausage and the pasta. Bring to the boil, then reduce the heat, cover and simmer for 10 minutes.

6 Serve in warm bowls.

🕑 30 minutes to prepare

Lentil, Bacon and Tomato Soup

Makes 2 servings

2 rashers (slices) of bacon, rinded and chopped
10 ml/2 tsp sunflower or vegetable oil
1 small onion, sliced
2 large tomatoes, chopped
600 ml/1 pt/2½ cups chicken stock, made with 1 stock cube
50 g/2 oz/⅓ cup red lentils
Salt and freshly ground black pepper

1 Fry (sauté) the bacon in a saucepan for 3–4 minutes, then lift out with a slotted spoon and reserve.

2 In the same saucepan, heat the oil and gently fry the onion for 2–3 minutes.

3 Add the chopped tomatoes, stock, lentils and seasoning and bring to the boil. Reduce the heat, cover and simmer for 45 minutes.

4 Taste and adjust the seasoning, then blend in a liquidiser or rub through a sieve (strainer) until smooth.

5 Reheat the soup in the saucepan, and serve it with the cooked bacon sprinkled on top.

🕐 1 hour to prepare

Tortellini and Vegetable Soup

Makes 2 servings
15 ml/1 tbsp olive oil
3 spring onions (scallions), chopped
1 carrot, finely chopped
1 celery stick, chopped
1 garlic clove, crushed
25 g/1 oz smoked streaky bacon or chorizo sausage, diced
25 g/1 oz/⅙ cup green lentils
750 ml/1¼ pts/3 cups ham or chicken stock
Salt and freshly ground black pepper
40 g/1½ oz tortellini
100 g/4 oz green vegetables, such as broccoli, courgettes (zucchini) or French (green) beans

1   Heat the oil in a saucepan. Add the onions, carrot, celery, garlic and bacon or chorizo. Cook over a moderate heat for 3–4 minutes.

2   Stir in the lentils and stock. Season with salt and pepper. Bring to the boil, then reduce the heat, cover and simmer for 10 minutes.

3   Add the tortellini and continue simmering for a further 10 minutes.

4   Add the green vegetables and simmer for 5 minutes until the vegetables are tender.

🕐 *30 minutes to prepare*

✶ Tortellini are little parcels of pasta stuffed with a variety of fillings, such as beef and mortadella, or spinach and ricotta cheese. Added to soup, they make a really filling meal.

Creamy Mushrooms on Toast

25 g/1 oz/2 tbsp butter or margarine, plus extra for spreading
2–3 spring onions (scallions), finely chopped
15 ml/1 tbsp lemon juice
75 g/3 oz mushrooms, sliced
5 ml/1 tsp cornflour (cornstarch)
120 ml/4 fl oz/½ cup crème fraîche
5 ml/1 tsp curry paste
Salt and freshly ground black pepper
1 slice of wholemeal bread
2 sprigs of parsley, to garnish

1 Melt the butter or margarine in a saucepan, add the onions and fry (sauté) gently until soft.

2 Add the lemon juice and mushrooms and cook gently for 3 minutes.

3 Stir in the cornflour and cook, stirring, for 1 minute.

4 Gradually add the crème fraîche and cook gently for a few minutes until thickened, without allowing the soup to boil.

5 Add the curry paste and season to taste with salt and pepper.

6 Toast and butter the bread, then top with the mushroom mixture. Garnish with fresh parsley sprigs.

🕐 10 minutes to prepare

✻ Cap or button mushrooms are suitable for this recipe, or you could try some of the more unusual varieties that are now readily available, such as Swiss or Roman brown mushrooms, which have a firmer texture and a nutty flavour.

Cheese and Salmon Toasts

50 g/2 oz/½ cup Cheddar cheese, grated
90 g/3½ oz/1 small can of salmon, drained and mashed
15 ml/1 tbsp plain yoghurt
15 ml/1 tbsp lemon juice
Paprika, to taste
Salt and freshly ground black pepper
1 egg, beaten
2 slices of wholemeal bread

1 Put the grated cheese, salmon, yoghurt and lemon juice in a mixing bowl. Season to taste with paprika, salt and pepper. Beat well until mixed, then beat in the egg.

2 Toast the bread and place in a flameproof dish. Spoon the cheese mixture on top of the toast.

3 Place under a preheated low grill (broiler) for 10 minutes to heat through, then increase the heat and grill (broil) briefly to brown the top.

🕐 15 minutes to prepare

Italian Scrambled Eggs

2 eggs
30 ml/2 tbsp milk
Salt and freshly ground black pepper
25 g/1 oz/2 tbsp butter or margarine, plus extra for spreading
½ green (bell) pepper, chopped
1 shallot, chopped
3 button mushrooms, sliced
25 g/1 oz peperoni sausage, chopped
1–2 slices of wholemeal bread

1 Break the eggs into a bowl, add the milk and season with salt and pepper. Beat well with a fork.

2 Melt the butter or margarine in a saucepan and gently fry (sauté) the pepper, onion and mushrooms for 3 minutes.

3 Meanwhile, toast the bread.

4 Add the peperoni sausage to the saucepan, then pour in the beaten eggs and cook gently, stirring all the time until the egg is thick and creamy.

5 Butter the toast and serve with the scrambled eggs.

🕐 10 minutes to prepare

French Bread Pizza

½ small French loaf
1 tomato, sliced
2 slices of ham
4 slices of Cheddar cheese
5 ml/1 tsp dried mixed herbs

1 Split the French bread in half lengthways.

2 Arrange slices of tomato, ham and cheese on both halves of the bread and sprinkle with mixed herbs.

3 Cook under a hot grill (broiler) for a few minutes until the cheese is browned and bubbling.

🕐 10 minutes to prepare

✳ This makes a substantial snack that is a cross between cheese on toast and a pizza. You can use pittas instead of French bread, if you prefer.

Bagel with Smoked Salmon

1 plain or savoury onion bagel
25 g/1 oz/2 tbsp cream cheese
5 ml/1 tsp lemon juice
1 spring onion (scallion), chopped
Freshly ground black pepper
25 g/1 oz smoked salmon, thinly sliced

1 Halve the bagel and toast it.

2 Mix the cream cheese, lemon juice and spring onion together, and season with plenty of black pepper. Spread over the toasted bagel.

3 Top with the smoked salmon.

5 minutes to prepare

✳ Bagels, both plain and flavoured varieties, are now readily available in supermarkets.

Banana Bagel

1 plain or cinnamon bagel
1 banana
5 ml/1 tsp clear honey or maple syrup
A pinch of ground cinnamon
15 ml/1 tbsp plain yoghurt

1   Split the bagel, place under a hot grill (broiler) and toast the outer sides.

2   Mash together the banana, honey or maple syrup and cinnamon. Spread over the bagel halves and put back under the grill for 1 minute, until golden and bubbling.

3   Top with the yoghurt.

5 minutes to prepare

✷ This is delicious for breakfast – or at any other time of the day.

Fresh Fruit Bagel

1 plain or cinnamon bagel
25 g/1 oz/2 tbsp cream cheese
5 ml/1 tsp clear honey
A pinch of ground cinnamon
Fresh fruit

1   Halve the bagel and toast on both sides.

2   Mix together the cream cheese and honey. Spread over the toasted bagel.

3   Sprinkle with cinnamon and top with fresh fruit of your choice.

5 minutes to prepare

✸   Use any fresh fruit of your choice as a topping – strawberries, raspberries, cherries, or something more exotic, such as mangoes or kiwi fruit.

Ham and Egg Muffin

1 egg
1 English muffin
1 tomato, sliced
1–2 rocket or lettuce leaves
25 g/1 oz lean ham, sliced
15 ml/1 tbsp crème fraîche
5 ml/1 tsp Dijon mustard
Freshly ground black pepper

1   Bring a pan of lightly salted water to the boil and crack in the egg. Remove from the heat and allow to stand for 2 minutes.

2   Meanwhile, halve and toast the muffin.

3   Arrange the sliced tomato and salad leaves on one half of the muffin. Top with the ham and cooked egg.

4   Mix together the crème fraîche and mustard. Season well with pepper and spoon on to the egg.

5   Top with the other muffin half.

🕐 5 minutes to prepare

✱   You can use a large roll instead of a muffin for this simple recipe.

Stuffed Ciabatta

½ ciabatta loaf
1 small courgette (zucchini), thinly sliced
½ red onion, thinly sliced
½ red (bell) pepper, seeded and thinly sliced
5 ml/1 tsp olive oil
15 ml/1 tbsp crème fraîche
2.5 ml/½ tsp pesto

1 Cut the ciabatta in half lengthways.

2 Place the vegetables on a baking (cookie) sheet, drizzle over the olive oil and put under a hot grill (broiler) for about 7 minutes until the vegetables are tender and slightly charred.

3 Mix together the crème fraîche and pesto and spread over the cut sides of the bread.

4 Top with the vegetables and sandwich the two halves together.

🕐 8 minutes to prepare

✶ Ciabatta is an Italian bread made with olive oil and garlic, sometimes containing sun-dried tomatoes and basil. You can use it to make sandwiches with cold meats, cheese or salad, or stuff it with this wonderful hot vegetable filling.

Bruschetta

½ ciabatta loaf
45 ml/3 tbsp olive oil
1 garlic clove, crushed
1 tomato, chopped
15 ml/1 tbsp chopped fresh parsley
2–3 spring onions (scallions), chopped
Salt and freshly ground black pepper
100 g/4 oz mushrooms
30 ml/2 tbsp white wine

1 Cut the ciabatta in half lengthways.

2 Mix the olive oil and garlic.

3 Mix the tomato, parsley and spring onions. Season with salt and pepper.

4 Put the mushrooms on a grill (broiler) tray and brush with the olive oil mixture. Sprinkle on the wine and grill (broil) for 4–5 minutes until cooked through. Remove from the grill.

5 Brush the remaining olive oil over the pieces of ciabatta bread and toast under the grill.

6 Arrange the mushrooms on the toasted ciabatta and spoon the tomato mixture on top. Place under the hot grill for 1–2 minutes.

⌚ 10 minutes to prepare

✱ You can add all kinds of different toppings to ciabatta bread to make bruschetta. This recipe uses ordinary field mushrooms but you could try the more expensive Italian porcini mushrooms.

Stuffed Pitta

15 ml/1 tbsp sunflower or vegetable oil
50 g/2 oz/½ cup cooked chicken, diced
75 g/3 oz button mushrooms, sliced
½ small red (bell) pepper, sliced
2.5 ml/½ tsp chilli powder
15 ml/1 tbsp soy sauce
2.5 ml/½ tsp sugar
Salt and freshly ground black pepper
1 carrot, grated
50 g/2 oz cabbage, thinly sliced
1 pitta bread

1 Heat the oil in a frying pan (skillet) and fry (sauté) the chicken, mushrooms and pepper for 2 minutes, stirring occasionally.

2 Mix the chilli powder with the soy sauce and sugar, and season with salt and pepper. Add to the chicken mixture with the carrot and cabbage. Cook over a high heat for 2 minutes, stirring all the time.

3 Toast the pitta bread, or warm in the oven or under a grill (broiler).

4 Using a sharp knife, make a slit along one edge of the pitta and open up to form a pocket. Spoon the chicken and vegetable mixture into the pocket.

🕐 10 minutes to prepare

Eggs and Cheese

If you keep a few eggs and some cheese in the fridge, you need never be at a loss for ideas for a quick meal. Eggs will have a 'best before' date stamped on the box, so you can always check that they are still fresh. Cheese will keep in the refrigerator for up to a week, wrapped in clingfilm (plastic wrap) or foil, or in a plastic container.

Eggs have a very high food value they contain protein, as well as vitamins A, B, D, and iron and calcium in the yolk. Cheese is also rich in protein, so is an excellent substitute for meat in vegetarian dishes. It is a good source of calcium and vitamin A. But slimmers beware, most cheeses are also high in fat.

The following dishes are all substantial enough to be a main meal, eaten with some crusty bread and perhaps a fresh salad.

Italian Frittata

1 courgette (zucchini)
Salt and freshly ground black pepper
2 eggs
15 ml/1 tbsp milk
15 ml/1 tbsp sunflower or vegetable oil
1 small onion, sliced
50 g/2 oz button mushrooms

1 Cut the courgette into 1 cm/½ in slices, put into a sieve (strainer) and sprinkle with a little salt. Leave to drain for 15 minutes, then pat dry with kitchen paper (paper towels).

2 Break the eggs into a bowl, add the milk and season with salt and pepper. Beat well with a fork.

3 Heat the oil in a frying pan (skillet) and gently fry (sauté) the courgette slices, onion and mushrooms for 5 minutes.

4 Pour the beaten eggs into the pan and cook gently, stirring with a fish slice, until the egg is set but still a little moist.

5 Slide the frying pan under a hot grill (broiler) and cook until the top of the frittata is golden brown.

🕑 25 minutes to prepare

✴ This classic Italian dish should be baked in the oven, but this is a simpler and quicker variation, finished off under the grill (broiler).

Spinach and Pine Nut Omelette

75 g/3 oz frozen spinach
15 g/½ oz/1 tbsp butter or margarine
15 ml/1 tbsp pine nuts
15 ml/1 tbsp raisins
2 eggs
30 ml/2 tbsp water

1 Cook the spinach according to the packet instructions.

2 Melt half the butter or margarine in a frying pan (skillet) and gently fry (sauté) the pine nuts and raisins for a few minutes until the nuts begin to brown. Add the cooked spinach and toss over a low heat.

3 In a medium-sized bowl, beat the eggs with the water. Fold in the spinach mixture.

4 Melt the remaining butter or margarine in the frying pan and pour in the egg mixture. Cook gently over a low heat for 4–5 minutes until set underneath but still moist in the centre.

5 Preheat the grill (broiler) to moderate. Place the frying pan under the grill and cook until the top is lightly browned.

🕐 15 minutes to prepare

33

Spanish Omelette

1 large potato, diced
1 small onion, diced
15 ml/1 tbsp sunflower or vegetable oil
Salt
2 eggs

1 Mix together the potato and onion.

2 Heat the oil in a frying pan (skillet), add the potato and onion mixture, sprinkle with salt and fry (sauté) gently for 15–20 minutes until soft but not crisp. Remove from the pan with a slotted spoon.

3 Beat the eggs and mix with the cooked potato and onion.

4 Heat a little more oil in the pan until it is smoking hot, then pour in the egg mixture.

5 Cook for 2–3 minutes, until the egg is set but still a little moist.

6 Slide the frying pan under a hot grill (broiler) and cook for a few minutes until the top of the omelette is golden brown.

🕐 30 minutes to prepare

✷ For speed, you can use leftover boiled potato from a previous meal. Cook the onions on their own for a few minutes until soft, then simply mix with the cooked potato and eggs and continue from step 4.

Piperade

2 eggs
Salt and freshly ground black pepper
15 ml/1 tbsp sunflower or vegetable oil
1 small onion, sliced
½ green (bell) pepper, seeded and sliced
1 garlic clove, chopped
1 tomato, sliced

1   Break the eggs into a mixing bowl, season with salt and pepper and beat with a fork.

2   Heat the oil in a frying pan (skillet) and cook the onion, green pepper and garlic for about 5 minutes until soft.

3   Add the tomatoes and continue cooking for a further 2–3 minutes.

4   Pour the beaten eggs into the frying pan and stir gently with a fish slice. Cook over a low heat until the eggs are set but still moist.

5   Slide the frying pan under a hot grill (broiler) and cook until the top is golden brown.

🕐 *15 minutes to prepare*

Pizza Omelette

2 eggs
Salt and freshly ground black pepper
10 ml/2 tsp cold water
25 g/1 oz/2 tbsp butter or margarine
1 small onion, sliced
5 ml/1 tsp tomato purée (paste)
A pinch of dried mixed herbs
2 rashers (slices) of bacon, rinded and diced
25 g/1 oz/¼ cup Cheddar cheese, grated

1   Break the eggs into a mixing bowl. Add a pinch of salt and
pepper and the cold water and mix thoroughly with a fork. Put
to one side while you prepare the topping.

2   Melt the butter or margarine in a saucepan and cook the onion
gently for 4–5 minutes until soft. Add the tomato purée and
mixed herbs and cook for 1 minute. Remove from the heat and
set aside.

3   Heat a frying pan (skillet) and fry (sauté) the bacon pieces until
the fat runs and the bacon is browned. Lift out and keep on
one side.

4   Pour the beaten eggs into the still-hot frying pan. Stir gently
with a fish slice and continue cooking over a low heat until the
eggs are set underneath but still moist on top.

5   Remove from the heat and cover the omelette with the tomato
and onion mixture. Arrange the bacon pieces on top and
sprinkle with grated cheese.

6   Flash the omelette under a hot grill (broiler) to melt the cheese
and brown the top. Slide out of the pan on to a warm plate.

15–20 minutes to prepare

Tomato and Egg Tagine

2 eggs
10 ml/2 tsp olive oil
1 garlic clove, crushed
2–3 spring onions (scallions), chopped
2 tomatoes, chopped
100 g/4 oz/1 cup quick-cook couscous
150 ml/¼ pt/⅔ cup boiling water
Salt and freshly ground black pepper
A pinch of ground cumin

1 Cook one of the eggs in boiling water for 5–6 minutes. Drain and cover with cold water until cool enough to handle. Peel off the shell and roughly chop the hard-boiled (hard-cooked) egg.

2 Heat the oil in a pan and add the garlic and spring onions. Cook gently for 5 minutes, then add the tomatoes. Continue cooking for a further 10 minutes, stirring occasionally.

3 Meanwhile, put the couscous in a bowl and pour over the boiling water. Leave to soak for about 5 minutes, stirring occasionally.

4 Beat the remaining egg and add to the tomato mixture in the pan. Season well with salt, pepper and cumin. Stir and allow to cook gently for 2–3 minutes, until the egg is not quite set.

5 Add the chopped egg and cook for 1 further minute.

6 Serve at once, with the couscous.

 20 minutes to prepare

Eggs Florentine

2 eggs
75 g/3 oz frozen spinach
15 g/½ oz/1 tbsp butter or margarine
15 g/½ oz/2 tbsp plain (all-purpose) flour
120 ml/4 fl oz/½ cup milk
25 g/1 oz/¼ cup Cheddar cheese, grated
1.5 g/¼ tsp made mustard
Salt and freshly ground black pepper
Toast, to serve

1 Cook the eggs in boiling water for 8 minutes. Plunge into cold water and remove the shells.

2 Meanwhile, cook the spinach according to the instructions on the packet.

3 Melt the butter or margarine in a saucepan and stir in the flour. Remove the pan from the heat and gradually stir in the milk, making sure there are no lumps.

4 Return the pan to the heat and bring the sauce to the boil, stirring continuously until thickened. Remove from the heat, stir in the cheese and mustard and season to taste.

5 Put the spinach into a flameproof dish and arrange the eggs on top. Pour over the cheese sauce and brown under a hot grill (broiler).

6 Serve with toast.

⊙ 15 minutes to prepare

Cheese and Potato Pie

2 potatoes, diced
15 g/½ oz/1 tbsp butter or margarine
15 ml/1 tbsp milk
Salt and freshly ground black pepper
50 g/2 oz/½ cup Cheddar cheese, grated
1 tomato, sliced

1 Cook the potatoes in boiling, salted water for 15–20 minutes, until soft. Drain and return to the pan.

2 Mash the potatoes, then mix in the butter or margarine, milk and a little salt and pepper. Beat until the potatoes are creamy.

3 Add half the grated cheese and spoon into a flameproof dish.

4 Sprinkle over the remaining cheese, then arrange the sliced tomato on top.

5 Place under a hot grill (broiler) and cook until the top is golden brown.

🕐 30 minutes to prepare

✶ If you use leftover cooked potatoes, this dish will take only 10 minutes to prepare.

Eggs and Leeks au Gratin

2 eggs
25 g/1 oz/2 tbsp butter or margarine
2 leeks, chopped
15 g/½ oz/2 tbsp plain (all-purpose) flour
120 ml/4 fl oz/½ cup milk
50 g/2 oz/½ cup Cheddar cheese, grated
1.5 ml/¼ tsp made mustard
Salt and freshly ground black pepper

1 Cook the eggs in boiling water for 8 minutes. Plunge into cold water and remove the shells.

2 Meanwhile, melt half the butter or margarine in a frying pan (skillet) and cook the leeks gently for 5 minutes.

3 To make the cheese sauce, melt the remaining butter or margarine in a saucepan and stir in the flour. Remove the pan from the heat and gradually add the milk, stirring to ensure there are no lumps. Return to the heat and bring to the boil, stirring continuously until thickened. Remove from the heat, stir in half the cheese and all the mustard and season to taste.

4 Put the leeks into a flameproof dish. Halve the eggs and arrange on top of the leeks, rounded side up. Pour over the cheese sauce. Sprinkle the remaining grated cheese on top.

5 Put under a hot grill (broiler) until nicely browned.

 20 minutes to prepare

Ham and Cheese Pizza

100 g/4 oz/1 cup self-raising (self-rising) flour
Salt and freshly ground black pepper
30 ml/2 tbsp vegetable or sunflower oil
30 ml/2 tbsp water
30 ml/2 tbsp tomato purée (paste)
200 g/7 oz/1 small can of chopped tomatoes
50 g/2 oz/½ cup cooked ham, cut into strips
50 g/2 oz/½ cup Cheddar cheese, grated
5 ml/1 tsp dried mixed herbs

1   Put the flour into a mixing bowl with a little salt and pepper. Make a well in the centre of the flour and pour in 15 ml/1 tbsp of the oil and 15 ml/1 tbsp of the water. Mix to a soft dough.

2   On a floured surface, roll out the dough to a round that will fit your frying pan (skillet).

3   Heat a little of the remaining oil in the frying pan. Fry (sauté) the dough on one side for about 5 minutes, until the base is cooked and lightly brown. Turn out on to a plate.

4   Add the last of the oil to the frying pan and slide the dough back in, cooked side upwards.

5   Spread over the tomato purée, then top with the tomatoes, ham and grated cheese. Sprinkle with dried mixed herbs.

6   Cook until the underside is browned, and then cook under a hot grill (broiler) until the cheese on top is bubbling.

⏲ 15 minutes to prepare

Seafood

Fish and other seafood are delicious, versatile and extremely nutritious, being high in protein and low in fats. Most supermarkets now have a good fish counter, where you can buy single fish or fillets, which are ideal for one-person catering, as they are so quick to cook. If you ever thought fish was boring, just try some of these tasty recipes.

Simple Ways with Fish

The methods given below will cook fish fillets and steaks to moist and succulent perfection with the minimum of time and effort. Beware of overcooking, however – the results will be dry and disappointing.

Grilled (broiled) fish

Heat the grill (broiler). Put a knob of butter or margarine in a flameproof dish and put it under the grill to melt. Remove the dish and place the fish in it, skin-side down if it is a fillet. Spoon a little of the melted butter or margarine over the fish, and season with salt and pepper. Put the dish back under the heat for 5–6 minutes, until the fish is cooked (the flesh will flake when you prod it with a fork).

🕐 8 minutes to prepare

Poached fish

Put ½ cup milk and ½ cup water into a saucepan and bring it to the boil. Add a fillet of fish, reduce the heat and cover with a lid. Simmer for 5–6 minutes, until the fish flakes when you prod it with a fork.

🕐 8 minutes to prepare

Fish with cheese sauce

Grill (broil) or poach a fillet of white fish, such as cod, haddock, plaice or whiting, and serve with cheese sauce (see page 40).

🕐 10 minutes to prepare

Swordfish Steak with Tomato Sauce

1 tomato
15 g/½ oz/1 tbsp butter or margarine
10 g/¼ oz/1 tbsp flour
150 ml/¼ pt/⅔ cup milk
Salt and freshly ground black pepper
2.5 ml/½ tsp tomato purée (paste)
15 ml/1 tbsp chopped fresh parsley
1 swordfish steak
5 ml/1 tsp lemon juice
A sprig of parsley, to garnish
New potatoes and French (green) beans, to serve

1   Immerse the tomato in boiling water for 15–30 seconds, then skin. Cut the flesh into strips, discarding the seeds.

2   Melt half the butter or margarine in a small pan, stir in the flour and cook for 1 minute. Gradually add the milk and bring to the boil, stirring constantly. Simmer for 2 minutes. Season to taste, and add the tomato purée and parsley.

3   Dot the remaining butter or margarine on the fish steak and grill (broil) for 5–6 minutes on each side.

4   Add the tomato strips and lemon juice to the sauce and reheat. Spoon over the fish and garnish with parsley.

5   Serve with new potatoes and French beans.

🕐 15 minutes to prepare

✶ Swordfish is expensive, but any fish steak – for example, cod – can be used for this recipe.

Spicy Plaice

15 ml/1 tbsp plain yoghurt
5 ml/1 tsp tandoori or tikka paste
5 ml/1 tsp sunflower or vegetable oil
A pinch of salt
175–225g/6–8 oz plaice fillet
Plain rice and a green salad, to serve

1 Mix the yoghurt, paste, oil and salt together.

2 Lay the plaice fillet on the grill (broiler) pan and brush with the spicy yoghurt mixture.

3 Cook under a medium grill (broiler) for 4–5 minutes.

4 Serve with rice and a green salad.

⏱ 5 minutes to prepare

Tuna Steak with Pesto and Tomato

1 tuna steak
15 ml/1 tbsp olive oil
30 ml/2 tbsp dry white wine
Salt and freshly ground black pepper
1 tomato
A little sunflower or vegetable oil
5 ml/1 tsp lemon juice
10 ml/2 tsp pesto
15 ml/1 tbsp thick plain yoghurt
New potatoes and broccoli, to serve

1 Put the tuna steak in a small dish. Mix together the olive oil and wine. Season with salt and pepper and pour over the fish. Leave for 5 minutes.

2 Meanwhile, cut the tomato into three thick slices and season with salt and pepper. Heat a little sunflower or vegetable oil in a small pan and cook the tomato on both sides until golden brown.

3 Heat a non-stick frying pan (skillet). Cook the tuna steak for 2 minutes on one side, then turn and cook for a further 2 minutes.

4 Place the cooked fish on a warm plate, sprinkle with the lemon juice and arrange the tomato slices on top.

5 Stir the pesto into the yoghurt and spoon over the fish. Serve with new potatoes and broccoli.

🕐 15 minutes to prepare

Cod and Prawns in Lemon and Ginger Sauce

175 g/6 oz cod fillet
120 ml/4 fl oz/½ cup milk
15 g/½ oz/1 tbsp butter or margarine
1 cm/½ in piece of fresh ginger, peeled and grated
15 g/½ oz/2 tbsp plain (all-purpose) flour
60 ml/4 tbsp vegetable stock
15 ml/1 tbsp lemon juice
2.5 ml/½ tsp brown sugar
Salt and freshly ground black pepper
15 g/1 oz cooked peeled prawns (shrimp)
New potatoes and French (green) beans, to serve

1 Put the cod into a pan with 45 ml/3 tbsp of the milk and bring to the boil. Reduce the heat and simmer gently for 4–5 minutes, until the fish is cooked.

2 Meanwhile, melt the butter or margarine in a saucepan, add the ginger and cook for 1 minute. Stir in the flour and cook for 1 minute. Slowly add the remaining milk and stock, then bring to the boil, stirring all the time until thick and smooth.

3 Reduce the heat and add the lemon juice, sugar, and salt and pepper to taste. Stir in the prawns and cook for a few minutes until heated through.

4 Transfer the cooked fish to a warm plate, pour the sauce over and serve with new potatoes and French beans.

🕒 10 minutes to prepare

Spicy Fish and Beans

5 ml/1 tsp sunflower or vegetable oil
½ celery stick, finely chopped
½ onion, finely chopped
1 garlic clove, crushed
2 tomatoes, chopped
200 g/7 oz/1 small can of butter (lima) beans
1.5 ml/¼ tsp chilli powder
60 ml/4 tbsp dry white wine
175 g/6 oz cod or haddock fillet
15 ml/1 tbsp chopped fresh parsley
Freshly ground black pepper
Plain rice, to serve

1 Heat the oil in a pan and add the celery, onion and garlic. Cook for 5 minutes.

2 Add the tomatoes, beans and chilli powder. Simmer, uncovered, for 10 minutes.

3 Meanwhile, heat the wine in a pan, add the fish and poach gently for 4–5 minutes, until just cooked through.

4 Gently add the fish, together with the cooking liquid, to the tomato and bean mixture. Sprinkle with the parsley and season with pepper to taste.

5 Serve with rice.

⏱ 15 minutes to prepare

✴ Make this spicy fish as hot as you like by increasing the amount of chilli powder.

Cod with Lime and Coriander

175–225 g/6–8 oz cod fillet
25 g/1 oz/¼ cup plain (all-purpose) flour
Salt and freshly ground black pepper
1 garlic clove, crushed
5 ml/1 tsp made mustard
Juice and grated rind of 1 lime
30 ml/2 tbsp olive oil, plus extra for cooking
15 ml/1 tbsp chopped fresh coriander (cilantro)
New potatoes and mangetout (snow peas), to serve

1 Remove the skin from the cod fillet and wipe the fish with kitchen paper (paper towels).

2 Put the flour on to a plate, season with salt and pepper, then coat the fish, pressing well on both sides.

3 Mix together the garlic, mustard, lime juice and rind, olive oil and coriander. Season with salt and pepper.

4 Heat a little olive oil in a frying pan (skillet), then add the fish fillet and fry (sauté) for 3 minutes on each side, until crisp and golden.

5 Pour the lime mixture around the fish and continue cooking for another 2–3 minutes.

6 Serve with new potatoes and mangetout.

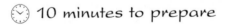 10 minutes to prepare

49

Cod with Green Pepper

15 ml/1 tbsp sunflower or vegetable oil
½ green (bell) pepper, chopped
175–225 g/6–8 oz cod fillet
120 ml/4 fl oz/½ cup passata (sieved tomatoes)
15 ml/1 tbsp lemon juice
5 ml/1 tsp Worcestershire sauce
Salt and freshly ground black pepper
Plain rice or potatoes and a green salad, to serve

1 Heat the oil in a frying pan (skillet) and cook the green pepper for 3 minutes.

2 Move it to one side of the pan and add the cod fillet.

3 Cook the fish on both sides until lightly browned.

4 Add the passata, lemon juice and Worcestershire sauce. Season with salt and pepper.

5 Cover with a lid (use a plate if the frying pan does not have one) and cook over a low heat for 5 minutes, until the fish flakes easily with a fork.

6 Serve with plain rice or potatoes and a green salad.

🕐 10 minutes to prepare

Sesame Plaice

15 g/½ oz/1 tbsp butter or margarine
175–225 g/6–8 oz plaice fillet
3 spring onions (scallions), chopped
10 ml/2 tsp lemon juice
5 ml/1 tsp sesame seeds
Salt and freshly ground black pepper
Plain rice and a tomato salad, to serve

1 Melt the butter or margarine in a saucepan.

2 Fold the plaice fillet in half, and put it into the saucepan with the chopped spring onions.

3 Cover and cook gently for 3–4 minutes, turning once.

4 Add the lemon juice and sesame seeds and season with salt and pepper.

5 Cook for 1 minute.

6 Serve with rice and a tomato salad.

⏱ 5 minutes to prepare

Smoked Haddock and Egg Mornay

50–75 g/2–3 oz smoked haddock fillet
150 ml/¼ pint/⅔ cup milk
1 egg
15 g/½ oz/1 tbsp butter or margarine
15 g/½ oz/2 tbsp plain (all-purpose) flour
25 g/1 oz/¼ cup Cheddar cheese, grated
Freshly ground black pepper
Sprigs of parsley, to garnish
Boiled potatoes and steamed courgettes (zucchini), to serve

1 Place the haddock fillet in a pan with the milk. Cook gently for about 10 minutes, until the flesh is beginning to flake.

2 Using a fish slice, transfer the cooked fish to a flameproof serving dish and keep warm. Reserve the milk.

3 Meanwhile, cook the egg in an egg poacher (or in a pan of simmering water) for 5 minutes, until set. Place on top of the haddock fillet in the serving dish.

4 Melt the butter or margarine in a small saucepan. Stir in the flour and cook, stirring, for 2 minutes. Blend in the reserved milk and simmer, stirring, until thickened. Stir in two-thirds of the cheese.

5 Pour the cheese sauce over the fish and egg. Sprinkle over the remaining cheese and season with pepper to taste.

6 Place under a hot grill (broiler) until lightly browned.

7 Garnish with sprigs of parsley and serve with boiled potatoes and steamed courgettes.

 20 minutes to prepare

Italian-style Whiting

1 whiting fillet
5 ml/1 tsp lemon juice
75 g/3 oz pasta shells
1 quantity of Spicy Tomato Sauce (see page 99)
A green salad, to serve

1 Put the whiting fillet into a saucepan with a little water and the lemon juice. Bring to the boil, then reduce the heat and cover with a lid. Simmer for 5–6 minutes, until the fish flakes when you prod it with a fork.

2 Meanwhile, cook the pasta according to the instructions on the packet.

3 Make the Spicy Tomato Sauce.

4 Place the whiting on a warm plate with the pasta, pour over the sauce and serve with a green salad.

 10 minutes to prepare

Salmon with Yoghurt and Tarragon

175 g/6 oz salmon steak or fillet
15 ml/1 tbsp chopped fresh tarragon
A dash of white wine vinegar
15 ml/1 tbsp plain yoghurt
New potatoes and broccoli, to serve

1 Bring a pan of lightly salted water to the boil. Put in the fish and simmer gently for 3 minutes, until cooked.

2 Remove the fish from the water and put on a plate.

3 Stir the tarragon and vinegar into the yoghurt and spoon on top of the fish.

4 Serve with new potatoes and broccoli.

⏲ 5 minutes to prepare

Japanese-style Salmon Teriyaki with Noodles

175 g/6 oz salmon fillet
½ red (bell) pepper, thinly sliced
2.5 ml/½ tsp fresh root ginger, finely chopped
45 ml/3 tbsp teriyaki sauce
75 g/3 oz medium egg noodles
2 spring onions (scallions), finely chopped

1 Place the salmon, sliced pepper and ginger in a shallow dish and pour over the teriyaki sauce. Leave to marinate for 15 minutes.

2 Remove the salmon from the marinade, leaving the peppers and ginger. Put the salmon into a hot frying pan (skillet), skin-side down. Fry (sauté) for 5 minutes, then turn the fillet, add the peppers and ginger and cook for a further 5 minutes. Reserve the marinade.

3 Meanwhile, place the egg noodles in a large pan of boiling water, then reduce the heat and simmer for 4 minutes. Drain and rinse under cold running water.

4 Remove the salmon and peppers from the pan, pour in the reserved marinade and boil for 1 minute. Stir in the noodles.

5 Serve garnished with chopped spring onions.

🕐 15 minutes to prepare, plus marinating

✱ You can buy teriyaki sauce in a bottle. Alternatively, make your own version by mixing together equal parts pale dry sherry and soy sauce, and a finely chopped garlic clove.

Thai Prawns and Noodles

75 g/3 oz rice noodles
1 green chilli, seeded and chopped
15 ml/2 tbsp chopped fresh coriander (cilantro)
Juice of 1 lime
2 spring onions (scallions), finely chopped
2 lemongrass stems, finely shredded
5 ml/1 tsp fish sauce
100 g/4 oz cooked peeled prawns (shrimp)
Salt and freshly ground black pepper

1 Cook the rice noodles according to the packet instructions.

2 Mix together all the remaining ingredients and season to taste.

3 Put the cooked noodles on to a serving plate and spoon over the prawn mixture.

🕐 10 minutes to prepare

Prawn Chow Mein

75 g/3 oz medium egg noodles
15 ml/1 tbsp sunflower or vegetable oil
1 garlic clove, finely chopped
2–3 spring onions (scallions), thinly sliced
2.5 ml/½ tsp chopped fresh root ginger
100 g/4 oz mixed vegetables, thinly sliced
100 g/4 oz beansprouts
100 g/4 oz cooked peeled prawns (shrimp)
15 ml/1 tbsp soy sauce
5 ml/1 tsp sesame oil

1 Put the noodles into a large pan of boiling water. Bring back to the boil, reduce the heat and simmer for 4 minutes. Drain and rinse under cold running water.

2 Heat the oil in a wok or large frying pan (skillet). Add the garlic, spring onions and ginger. Stir-fry for 2 minutes.

3 Add the vegetables and stir-fry for 3 minutes.

4 Stir in the cooked noodles, prawns, soy sauce and sesame oil. Continue cooking for another 2 minutes to heat through.

15 minutes to prepare

★ Courgettes (zucchini), mangetout (snow peas) and (bell) peppers are all good choices for the mixed vegetables in this recipe.

Gingered Prawn Stir-fry

100 g/4 oz frozen prawns (shrimp), thawed
25 g/1 oz/¼ cup cornflour (cornstarch)
A pinch of salt
½ egg white
15 ml/1 tbsp dry sherry
15 ml/1 tbsp sunflower or vegetable oil
5 ml/1 tsp grated fresh root ginger
25 g/1 oz peas
15 ml/1 tbsp vegetable stock or water
A few drops of sesame oil
Rice or noodles, to serve

1   Put the prawns into a bowl and sprinkle with half the cornflour and a pinch of salt. Stir in the egg white and sherry.

2   Heat the sunflower or vegetable oil in a wok or frying pan (skillet) and add the grated ginger.

3   Add the prawns and stir-fry until they turn pink, then add the peas and stir-fry for 3–4 minutes.

4   Blend the remaining cornflour with the stock and sesame oil and add this sauce to the pan.

5   Continue cooking for 1–2 minutes until the sauce is slightly thickened and translucent.

6   Serve with rice or noodles.

🕐 10 minutes to prepare

Seafood Kebabs

175 g/6 oz fillet of cod or haddock
½ green (bell) pepper
50 g/2 oz peeled prawns (shrimp)
6–8 button mushrooms
A little sunflower or vegetable oil or melted butter or margarine
Salt and freshly ground black pepper
A dash of lemon juice
Plain rice, to serve
Slices of lemon, to garnish

1 Cut the fish and green pepper into neat pieces. Push the cod, peppers, prawns and mushrooms alternately on to two skewers.

2 Brush with oil or melted butter or margarine, and season lightly with salt and pepper. Sprinkle with lemon juice.

3 Cook under a hot grill (broiler) for 8–10 minutes, turning several times.

4 Serve the kebabs on a bed of rice garnished with slices of lemon.

🕐 10 minutes to prepare

Chicken

Individual chicken joints make excellent, tasty meals for one and you have a choice of breast, thigh, leg or drumsticks. Boned chicken breasts are particularly convenient because they are so quick to cook, and there is no waste.

If you buy a frozen joint, you can speed up the defrosting process by immersing it under cold running water. Never use hot water – germs thrive in warm conditions and chicken is particularly susceptible to nasty bacteria.

Coriander and Lime Chicken

1 lime
15 ml/1 tbsp chopped fresh coriander (cilantro)
1 garlic clove, crushed
15 ml/1 tbsp dry white wine
15 ml/1 tbsp olive oil
5 ml/1 tsp clear honey
Salt and freshly ground black pepper
1 boneless chicken breast
2–3 spring onions (scallions), chopped
New potatoes and French (green) beans, to serve

1 Halve the lime and cut one half into slices, then reserve for garnishing. Squeeze the juice from the other half, and grate the rind.

2 Mix together the lime juice and rind, half the coriander, the garlic, wine, olive oil and honey. Season well.

3 Coat the chicken breast with the lime mixture. Line a grill (broiler) pan with foil and grill (broil) the chicken for 10–12 minutes on each side, basting with the lime mixture.

4 Put the chicken on a serving plate, pour over the juices, and sprinkle with the remaining coriander and the spring onions.

5 Garnish with the slices of lime, and serve with new potatoes and French beans.

 30 minutes to prepare

Mexican Chicken with Tortillas and Salsa

1 chicken breast, boned and skinned
Juice of ½ lime
10 ml/2 tsp sesame oil
1 garlic clove, cut in half
45 ml/3 tbsp chicken stock
Salt
A pinch of chilli powder
A few rocket leaves
A sprig of coriander (cilantro), to garnish
Corn tortillas and salsa, to serve

1 Cut the chicken breast lengthwise into strips 2.5 cm (1 in) wide. Place in a bowl, add the lime juice and toss gently.

2 Warm the oil in a frying pan (skillet). Add the garlic and cook gently for 1–2 minutes, until soft. Discard the garlic.

3 Add the chicken and cook, turning, until golden on both sides. Transfer to a plate and keep warm.

4 Add the chicken stock to the pan, bring to the boil and simmer until the liquid has been reduced by about one half, stirring continuously. Season with salt and chilli powder.

5 Arrange some rocket leaves on a serving plate and top with the chicken strips. Pour the warm sauce over the chicken. Garnish with a sprig of fresh coriander and the other half of the lime, sliced. Serve with warmed tortillas and salsa.

15 minutes to prepare

Lemon Chicken

1 boneless chicken breast
Salt and freshly ground black pepper
15 ml/1 tbsp sunflower or vegetable oil
15 ml/1 tbsp chicken stock
5 ml/1 tsp lemon juice
5 ml/1 tsp soy sauce
2 spring onions (scallions), chopped
Plain rice and stir-fried vegetables, to serve

1 Cut the chicken into thin strips and season it well with salt and pepper.

2 Heat the oil in a frying pan (skillet) and fry (sauté) the chicken quickly, stirring all the time, until it is golden brown.

3 Add the stock, lemon juice and soy sauce.

4 Stir in the spring onions and cook for 2–3 minutes.

5 Serve with rice and stir-fried vegetables.

 10 minutes to prepare

Chicken in Smoky Bacon Sauce

15 ml/1 tbsp sunflower or vegetable oil
1 chicken breast, boned and skinned
1 rasher (slice) of streaky bacon, chopped
60 ml/4 tbsp apple juice
5 ml/1 tsp chopped fresh thyme
OR 2.5 ml/½ tsp dried thyme
Salt and freshly ground black pepper
2–3 spring onions (scallions), chopped
1 red eating (dessert) apple, sliced
15 ml/1 tbsp crème fraîche
Noodles or pasta, to serve

1 Heat the oil in a pan. Add the chicken and bacon and fry (sauté) for about 5 minutes, until golden.

2 Stir in the apple juice and thyme, and season to taste. Bring to the boil, then reduce the heat, cover and simmer for 10 minutes.

3 Add the spring onions and apple and cook, uncovered, over a high heat for 5 minutes.

4 Turn down the heat and stir in the crème fraîche. Check the seasoning.

5 Serve with noodles or pasta.

⏱ *25 minutes to prepare*

Orange Chicken with Almonds

25 g/1 oz/2 tbsp butter or margarine
25 g/1 oz/2 tbsp flaked (slivered) almonds
1 chicken joint
Salt and freshly ground black pepper
A pinch of paprika
1 orange
5 ml/1 tsp sugar
Plain rice or noodles and a green salad, to serve

1 Melt the butter or margarine in a pan, add the almonds and fry (sauté) gently until golden. Remove with a slotted spoon and set aside.

2 Sprinkle the chicken joint with salt, pepper and paprika. Add to the fat remaining in the pan and fry until golden brown all over. Cover and cook gently for 25–30 minutes, until tender. Transfer to a serving dish and keep warm.

3 Peel and halve the orange. Squeeze the juice from one half and divide the other half into segments. Add the juice, segments and sugar to the pan juices and boil rapidly for 1–2 minutes. Pour over the cooked chicken.

4 Sprinkle with the almonds and serve with plain rice or noodles and a green salad.

🕐 35 minutes to prepare

One-pot Chicken and Potato

25 g/1 oz/¼ cup plain (all-purpose) flour
Salt and freshly ground black pepper
1 chicken joint
25 g/1 oz/2 tbsp butter or margarine
1 small onion, chopped
2 tomatoes, chopped
1 large potato, peeled and diced
2.5 ml/½ tsp dried mixed herbs
Broccoli or a green salad, to serve

1 In a shallow dish or a plate, mix the flour with a little salt and pepper. Dip the chicken in the flour so that it is coated on all sides.

2 Melt the butter or margarine in a saucepan and fry (sauté) the onion until it begins to soften.

3 Add the chicken and fry until golden brown on all sides.

4 Add the tomatoes, diced potato and herbs, and season with salt and pepper.

5 Cover with a lid and simmer over a low heat for about 25 minutes, until the chicken is tender.

6 Serve with broccoli or a green salad.

🕐 35 minutes to prepare

Herby Chicken and Rice

15 g/½ oz/1 tbsp butter or margarine
1 small onion, finely chopped
1 carrot, thinly sliced
1 chicken joint
100 g/4 oz/½ cup long-grain rice
2.5 ml/½ tsp dried mixed herbs
Salt and freshly ground black pepper
A green salad, to serve

1 Melt the butter or margarine in a saucepan and gently fry (sauté) the onion and carrot.

2 Add the chicken joint and brown it on all sides.

3 Add the rice and enough water to cover everything.

4 Add the herbs and season with salt and pepper.

5 Bring to the boil, then reduce the heat, cover with a lid and simmer for 40 minutes. (Check occasionally and add a little extra water if the mixture is looking too dry.)

6 Serve with a green salad.

🕐 45 minutes to prepare

Italian Chicken

15 ml/1 tbsp sunflower or vegetable oil
1 garlic clove, crushed
1 chicken breast, boned and skinned
½ small red (bell) pepper, chopped
½ small yellow pepper, chopped
200 g/7 oz/1 small can of chopped tomatoes
2.5 ml/½ tsp dried mixed herbs
Salt and freshly ground black pepper
Plain rice and a green salad, to serve

1 Heat the oil in a saucepan and fry (sauté) the crushed garlic for 1 minute.

2 Add the chicken breast and fry until browned on both sides.

3 Add the peppers, tomatoes and herbs. Season with salt and pepper.

4 Bring everything up to simmering point, then cook, uncovered, for 15 minutes.

5 Serve with rice and a green salad.

🕐 20 minutes to prepare

Chicken Kebabs

1 boneless chicken breast
30 ml/2 tbsp plain yoghurt
15 ml/1 tbsp clear honey
1 garlic clove, crushed
5 ml/1 tsp curry paste
½ yellow (bell) pepper, seeded and cubed
6 button mushrooms
Plain rice, to serve

1 Cut the chicken into cubes, and put it into a bowl with the yoghurt, honey, garlic and curry paste. Mix thoroughly and leave to stand for 30 minutes.

2 Push the chicken cubes on to a skewer, alternating with the yellow pepper and mushrooms.

3 Cook under a hot grill (broiler) for 15 minutes, turning frequently.

4 Serve on a bed of plain rice.

🕐 15 minutes to prepare, plus marinating

Chicken Kebabs and Peanut Sauce

2 rashers (slices) of streaky bacon
1 banana, cut into chunks
50–75 g/2–3 oz boneless chicken breast
5 ml/1 tsp clear honey
5 ml/1 tsp Worcester sauce
15 ml/1 tbsp lemon juice
1 garlic clove, crushed
15 ml/1 tbsp crunchy peanut butter
30 ml/2 tbsp orange juice
2 spring onions (scallions), chopped
A pinch of cayenne (optional)
Plain rice, to serve

1 Halve the bacon rashers lengthwise and wrap a strip round each chunk of banana.

2 Cut the chicken into bite-sized pieces and thread on to two skewers, alternating with the bacon-wrapped banana.

3 Mix the honey, Worcester sauce and lemon juice together and brush on to the kebabs.

4 Cook the kebabs under a hot grill (broiler), turning three or four times.

5 Combine all the remaining ingredients to make the sauce. Place the cooked kebabs on a bed of rice, and serve with the sauce.

 20 minutes to prepare

Chicken Paprika

1 chicken breast, skinned and boned
5 ml/1 tsp olive oil
10 ml/2 tsp lemon juice
2.5 ml/½ tsp paprika
Freshly ground black pepper
Plain rice and a green salad, to serve

1 Cut the chicken into bite-sized cubes and put them into a small bowl.

2 Mix together the olive oil, lemon juice, paprika and a good grinding of black pepper. Pour over the chicken and leave to marinate for 10 minutes.

3 Line the grill (broiler) pan with foil to catch the juices. Grill (broil) the chicken cubes for 10–12 minutes, turning them from time to time and basting them with the juices that drip into the foil.

4 Spoon the cooked chicken on to a bed of rice and pour the juices left in the foil over the top.

5 Serve with a salad.

🕐 15 minutes to prepare, plus marinating

Chicken Pilaff

½ cup long-grain rice
1 chicken stock cube
1 cup boiling water
25 g/1 oz/2 tbsp butter or margarine
1 small onion, sliced
75 g/3 oz/¾ cup cooked chicken, cut into strips
1 tomato, chopped
1.5 ml/¼ tsp dried thyme
Salt and freshly ground black pepper

1 Put the rice into a sieve (strainer) and rinse it thoroughly under cold running water until the water runs clear. Leave to drain.

2 Dissolve the stock cube in the boiling water.

3 Heat the butter or margarine in a saucepan and gently fry (sauté) the onion until it is transparent.

4 Add the cooked chicken to the saucepan and fry until it is lightly browned. Add the rice and continue cooking for 2 minutes, stirring all the time to stop it sticking to the pan. Add the tomato, chicken stock, thyme, salt and pepper.

5 Bring to the boil, then reduce the heat and simmer for 12–15 minutes, until all the water has been absorbed and the rice is soft.

🕐 *25 minutes to prepare*

✶ It doesn't matter what size of cup you use for the rice as long as you add double the quantity of water.

Chicken Chow Mein

75 g/3 oz medium egg noodles
15 ml/1 tbsp sunflower or vegetable oil
1 boneless chicken breast, skinned and thinly sliced
1 small onion, sliced
1 garlic clove, sliced
1 carrot, grated
175 g/6 oz beansprouts, fresh or canned
15 ml/1 tbsp light soy sauce
5 ml/1 tsp sesame oil
1.5 ml/¼ tsp sugar
Salt

1   Put the noodles into a saucepan of boiling water, remove from the heat and cover with a lid. Leave to stand.

2   Meanwhile, heat the sunflower or vegetable oil in a wok or frying pan (skillet), add the chicken and stir-fry for 2–3 minutes, until the chicken is white.

3   Add the onion, garlic and carrot, and stir-fry for another 2 minutes. Add the beansprouts, soy sauce, sesame oil, sugar and salt.

4   Drain the noodles into a sieve (strainer), then add to the chicken and beansprouts.

5   Mix everything together thoroughly and heat gently for a few minutes before serving.

 15 minutes to prepare

Thai Chicken and Noodles

1 chicken breast, skinned and boned
Grated rind and juice of 1 lime
5 ml/1 tsp sunflower or vegetable oil
1 garlic clove, thinly sliced
75 g/3 oz medium egg noodles
¼ cucumber, sliced
2 spring onions (scallions), sliced
15 ml/1 tbsp chopped fresh coriander (cilantro)
1.5 ml/¼ tsp chilli powder
2.5 ml/½ tsp clear honey

1   Place the chicken in a non-metallic dish. Spoon over half the lime juice and rind and leave to marinate for 30 minutes.

2   Heat the oil in a pan, add the chicken and garlic and fry (sauté) for 6–7 minutes, until the chicken is cooked through.

3   Meanwhile, cook the noodles in lightly salted, boiling water for 4 minutes. Drain and rinse under cold running water.

4   Mix together the cucumber, spring onions, coriander, chilli and noodles.

5   Mix the remaining lime juice and rind with the honey, and stir into the noodles. Spoon on to a serving plate.

6   Slice the cooked chicken and arrange on top of the noodles.

🕐 *10 minutes to prepare, plus marinating*

Chicken and Peppers

75–100 g/3–4 oz boneless chicken breast
15 ml/1 tbsp sunflower or vegetable oil
1 red, yellow or green (bell) pepper, diced
1 clove of garlic, sliced
15 ml/1 tbsp soy sauce
Plain rice, to serve

1 Remove the skin from the chicken and cut into bite-sized pieces.

2 Heat the oil in a frying pan (skillet) or wok. When it is really hot, add the chicken and stir-fry for 4–5 minutes, until the flesh is white.

3 Turn down the heat to moderate. Push the chicken to one side of the pan and put the pepper and garlic on the other side. Continue cooking for 3–4 minutes, then mix the chicken and pepper together and add the soy sauce.

4 Heat through for 1–2 minutes.

5 Serve with rice.

🕑 15 minutes to prepare

✳ This dish looks more attractive if you use two or three differently coloured peppers, but for one person it may be more economical to buy just one variety.

Chicken with Mushrooms and Broccoli

1 boneless chicken breast
10 ml/2 tsp cornflour (cornstarch)
10 ml/2 tsp soy sauce
15 ml/1 tbsp sunflower or vegetable oil
1 small onion, finely chopped
1 garlic clove, crushed
50 g/2 oz broccoli, divided into florets
50 g/2 oz button mushrooms
30 ml/2 tbsp sherry
Salt and freshly ground black pepper
Plain rice or noodles, to serve

1   Remove the skin from the chicken and cut into bite-sized pieces. Put the cornflour into a shallow dish and toss the chicken pieces in it. Sprinkle the soy sauce over the chicken and leave to stand for 20 minutes.

2   Heat the oil in a large frying pan (skillet) or wok and stir-fry the chicken for 2–3 minutes. Push the chicken to one side, turn down the heat and add the onion and garlic. Cook for a further 2 minutes.

3   Add the broccoli florets and the mushrooms. Continue stir-frying these for 1 minute, then mix all the ingredients together, drawing in the chicken from the side. Pour over the sherry and heat through for another couple of minutes.

4   Serve with rice or noodles.

🕐 10 minutes to prepare, plus marinating

Chicken with Rosemary

1 boneless chicken breast
5 ml/1 tsp sunflower or vegetable oil
A knob of butter or margarine
½ onion, sliced
½ red (bell) pepper, seeded and sliced
5 ml/1 tsp fresh chopped rosemary
OR 2.5 ml/½ tsp dried rosemary
75 g/3 oz/⅓ cup basmati rice
250 ml/8 fl oz/1 cup chicken stock

1   Cut the chicken breast into thin strips.

2   Heat the oil in a frying pan (skillet) or wok, add the chicken and stir-fry for about 5 minutes, or until beginning to brown. Transfer to a plate.

3   Melt the butter or margarine in the same pan, add the onion and red pepper, and cook for about 5 minutes, or until soft.

4   Add the rosemary and cook for 1 further minute. Return the chicken to the pan, add the rice and stir.

5   Pour the stock over the chicken and rice mixture and bring to the boil. Reduce the heat, cover with a tight-fitting lid and simmer gently for 20 minutes, or until the rice is tender and the liquid is absorbed.

🕑 35 minutes to prepare

Chicken Stir-fry with Ginger

1 boneless chicken breast
15 ml/1 tbsp sunflower or vegetable oil
½ onion, finely chopped
1 celery stick, finely chopped
1 cm/½ in piece of fresh root ginger, peeled and grated
1 garlic clove, crushed
½ red (bell) pepper, seeded and sliced
1 small carrot, cut into thin strips
1 small courgette (zucchini), thinly sliced
100 g/4 oz beansprouts
15 ml/1 tbsp dry sherry
5 ml/1 tsp soy sauce
Plain rice or noodles, to serve

1 Cut the chicken breast into thin strips.

2 Heat the oil in a wok or frying pan (skillet). Add the chicken, onion and celery and stir-fry for 2–3 minutes.

3 Add the ginger and garlic and stir-fry for 1 minute.

4 Add the pepper, carrot and courgette and stir-fry until they start to soften, then add the beansprouts.

5 Stir in the sherry and soy sauce. Cook for a further 2–3 minutes.

6 Serve with rice or noodles.

 10 minutes to prepare

Meat

Grilled (broiled) chops and steaks make good meals for one, and need not be boring if you vary the accompaniments. Stir-frying is also very quick and easy, but because the meat is cooked very quickly, you need to use a tender, good-quality cut. If you have time, it is a good idea to leave the meat to marinate and tenderise for 30 minutes or longer in some soy sauce or wine vinegar.

Beef Stir-fry with Noodles

75 g/3 oz medium egg noodles
15 ml/1 tbsp sunflower or vegetable oil
2 spring onions (scallions), chopped
1 garlic clove, crushed
1 small carrot, cut into matchsticks
½ green (bell) pepper, seeded and thinly sliced
100 g/4 oz rump, sirloin or fillet steak
60 ml/4 tbsp beef stock
15 ml/1 tbsp soy sauce
10 ml/2 tsp white wine vinegar
5 ml/1 tsp cornflour (cornstarch)
Salt and freshly ground black pepper
15 ml/1 tbsp sesame seeds

1 Cook the noodles according to the instructions on the packet.

2 Meanwhile, heat the oil in a frying pan (skillet) or wok and stir-fry the onions, garlic, carrot and green pepper for 2–3 minutes.

3 Cut the meat into thin strips and add to the vegetables. Continue stir-frying for another 5–6 minutes, until the meat is browned and tender.

4 Add the stock, soy sauce and vinegar and bring to the boil. Blend the cornflour with a little cold water and stir into the sauce to thicken it.

5 Season with salt and pepper, and mix with the noodles.

6 Sprinkle with sesame seeds before serving.

15 minutes to prepare

Beef in Oyster Sauce

100 g/4 oz rump, sirloin or fillet steak
15 ml/1 tbsp sunflower or vegetable oil
1 green (bell) pepper, seeded and thinly sliced
45 ml/3 tbsp oyster sauce
Plain rice, to serve

1   Cut the steak into thin strips.

2   Heat the oil in a frying pan (skillet) or wok. When it is really hot, add the sliced meat and fry (sauté) for 3 minutes, stirring all the time.

3   Add the sliced pepper and continue frying for 2 more minutes.

4   Turn the heat down and add the oyster sauce. Heat through gently for a further 5 minutes.

5   Serve with rice.

⏱ 15 minutes to prepare

✕ This is equally good with black bean sauce, which has a spicier flavour.

Minute Steak

1 minute steak
Garlic salt, to taste
Freshly ground black pepper
15 ml/1 tbsp sunflower or vegetable oil
15 g/½ oz/1 tbsp butter or margarine
2 spring onions (scallions), chopped
5 ml/1 tsp lemon juice
5 ml/1 tsp Worcester sauce
1.5 ml/¼ tsp made mustard
New potatoes and peas, to serve

1 Dust both sides of the steak with garlic salt and black pepper.

2 Heat the oil in a frying pan (skillet) and fry (sauté) the steak for 2 minutes on each side, on a medium heat.

3 Remove the steak from the frying pan and put it on a warmed plate.

4 Wipe out the pan with kitchen paper (paper towels), then melt the butter or margarine and add the chopped spring onions. Fry (sauté) gently for 2 minutes.

5 Add the lemon juice, Worcester sauce and mustard. Heat through gently, then pour the sauce over the steak.

6 Serve with new potatoes and peas.

🕐 10 minutes to prepare

Pork and Apple in Ginger Sauce

5 ml/2 tsp sunflower or vegetable oil
100 g/4 oz pork fillet, thinly sliced
1 eating (dessert) apple, sliced
1 cm/½ in piece of fresh root ginger, peeled and grated
25 g/1 oz/2 tbsp butter or margarine
Pasta or noodles, to serve

1 Heat the oil in a frying pan, add the sliced pork and fry (sauté) until it starts to brown.

2 Add the apple and ginger and cook for a further 5 minutes, until the apple starts to soften.

3 Add the butter or margarine and stir in until melted – take care not to allow it to burn.

4 Remove the pork and apple slices to a warmed serving dish and pour over the ginger sauce.

5 Serve with pasta or noodles.

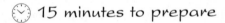 15 minutes to prepare

Paprika Pork

5 ml/2 tsp sunflower or vegetable oil
175 g/6 oz lean pork, cubed
1 small onion, finely chopped
1 garlic clove, crushed
5 ml/1 tsp paprika
A pinch of cayenne
Salt
200 g/7 oz/1 small can of tomatoes
15 ml/1 tbsp plain yoghurt
Plain rice or noodles and a green salad, to serve

1 Heat the oil in a saucepan until it is very hot and quicky fry (sauté) the cubed pork until it is browned. Remove from the saucepan.

2 In the same oil, fry the onion and garlic until soft.

3 Stir in the paprika, cayenne, a little salt and the tomatoes.

4 Return the meat to the pan and bring to the boil. Reduce the heat, cover and simmer for 30 minutes, until the pork is tender.

5 Remove from the heat and swirl in the yoghurt.

6 Serve with rice or noodles and a green salad.

🕐 35 minutes to prepare

Pork in Wine Sauce

25 g/1 oz/2 tbsp plain (all-purpose) flour
Salt and freshly ground black pepper
1 pork chop or steak
15 g/½ oz/1 tbsp butter or margarine
1 small onion, finely chopped
2.5 ml/½ tsp tomato purée (paste)
30 ml/2 tbsp white wine
Boiled potatoes and mangetout (snow peas), to serve

1 Mix the flour with a little salt and pepper on to a plate and coat the pork on both sides. Shake off any surplus flour.

2 Melt the butter or margarine in a saucepan and fry (sauté) the pork gently on both sides, until golden brown.

3 Remove the pork from the pan and add the onion. Cook gently until soft.

4 Return the pork to the pan and stir in the tomato purée and wine. Cover with a lid and cook over a low heat for 15–20 minutes, until the pork is tender.

5 Serve with boiled potatoes and mangetout.

🕐 35 minutes to prepare

Pork with Crunchy Red Cabbage

1 thin pork steak
15 ml/1 tbsp white wine vinegar
15 ml/1 tbsp chopped fresh mixed herbs
OR 5 ml/1 tsp dried mixed herbs
5 ml/1 tsp clear honey
10 ml/2 tsp lemon juice
Salt and freshly ground black pepper
5 ml/2 tsp sunflower or vegetable oil
1 small onion, chopped
50 g/2 oz red cabbage, shredded
1 small red eating (dessert) apple, chopped
Mashed potato or plain rice, to serve

1　Slash the pork steak with a knife in a criss-cross pattern.

2　Mix together the vinegar, herbs, honey, lemon juice and seasoning. Spoon over the pork steak and leave to marinate for 30 minutes.

3　Lift the steak from the marinade and put under a hot grill (broiler). Cook for 4–5 minutes on each side.

4　Meanwhile, heat the oil in a frying pan (skillet) and cook the onion for 2 minutes.

5　Add the shredded cabbage, chopped apple, and the remaining marinade mixture. Stir-fry over a moderate heat for 4–5 minutes, until the liquid has evaporated.

6　Serve the cooked pork steak with the red cabbage and mashed potato or rice.

🕐 20 minutes to prepare, plus marinating

Bacon Stir-fry

15 ml/1 tbsp sunflower or vegetable oil
50 g/2 oz bacon, rinded and diced
2–3 spring onions (scallions), chopped
5 ml/1 tsp grated fresh root ginger
1 carrot, cut into matchsticks
50 g/2 oz baby sweetcorn (corn)
50 g/2 oz broccoli florets
50 g/2 oz button mushrooms, sliced
15 ml/1 tbsp light soy sauce
Plain rice, to serve

1 Heat the oil in a wok or frying pan (skillet) and fry (sauté) the bacon until browned.

2 Add the onions and ginger and stir-fry for 1 minute.

3 Add the carrot, sweetcorn and broccoli and stir-fry for another 2–3 minutes.

4 Add the mushrooms and stir-fry for another 2–3 minutes, until the vegetables are tender but crisp.

5 Remove from the heat and stir in the soy sauce.

6 Serve with rice.

🕐 10 minutes to prepare

Stir-fried Pork with String Beans

100 g/4 oz lean pork steak
10 ml/2 tsp soy sauce
15 ml/1 tbsp sunflower or vegetable oil
5 ml/1 tsp grated fresh root ginger
1 garlic clove, crushed
Salt
50 g/2 oz string beans
1 small onion, sliced
5 ml/1 tsp sweet bean paste
5 ml/1 tsp cornflour (cornstarch)
Plain rice, to serve

1   Cut the pork into strips and put into a bowl with the soy sauce, half the oil, the ginger, garlic and a pinch of salt. Leave to marinate for 10 minutes.

2   String the beans and cut into lengths the same size as the pork strips. Cook in salted water for 3–4 minutes and then drain, reserving some of the cooking liquid.

3   Heat the remaining oil in a wok or frying pan (skillet) and fry (sauté) the onion for 1 minute. Remove with a slotted spoon and keep aside.

4   Add a little more oil to the pan, if necessary, and stir-fry the pork until it is browned. Add the onion and string beans.

5 Mix the sweet bean paste with 15 ml/1 tbsp of the reserved cooking liquid and blend in the cornflour. Add this to the pork mixture and cook until the sauce is thickened.

6 Serve with rice.

🕐 10 minutes to prepare, plus marinating

Glazed Gammon Steak

15 g/½ oz/1 tbsp butter or margarine
15 ml/1 tbsp clear honey
10 ml/2 tsp made mustard
Salt and freshly ground black pepper
175 g/6 oz gammon steak
New potatoes and peas, to serve

1 Put the butter or margarine into a flameproof dish, large enough to contain the gammon. Place under a hot grill (broiler) until melted.

2 Meanwhile mix the honey, mustard, salt and pepper together. Coat the gammon steak on both sides with this mixture.

3 Lay the gammon steak in the dish in which you have melted the butter or margarine, and grill (broil) for 5 minutes on each side.

4 Serve with new potatoes and peas.

🕐 10 minutes to prepare

Sweet and Sour Pork

100 g/4 oz lean pork, cubed
15 ml/1 tbsp white wine vinegar
15 ml/1 tbsp soy sauce
15 ml/1 tbsp sunflower or vegetable oil
1 small onion, chopped
½ green (bell) pepper, chopped
1 carrot, chopped
5 ml/1 tsp sugar
5 ml/1 tsp tomato purée (paste)
30 ml/2 tbsp pineapple juice
5 ml/1 tsp cornflour (cornstarch)
15 ml/1 tbsp water
Salt and freshly ground black pepper
Plain rice, to serve

1 Put the pork in a bowl with the vinegar and soy sauce. Mix thoroughly and leave to marinate for 30 minutes.

2 Lift the pork out of the marinade with a slotted spoon. Reserve the marinade.

3 Heat the oil in a wok or frying pan (skillet) and when it is really hot add the pork and stir-fry for 3 minutes. Add the vegetables and continue stir-frying for another 2 minutes.

4 Stir the sugar, tomato purée and pineapple juice into the reserved marinade. Mix the cornflour with the water and add to the mixture.

5 Pour over the pork and vegetables, season and bring to the boil. Reduce the heat and simmer for 1–2 minutes.

6 Serve with rice.

🕐 10 minutes to prepare, plus marinating

Shish Kebabs

175 g/6 oz boned lamb
15 ml/1 tbsp sunflower or vegetable oil
15 ml/1 tbsp white wine vinegar
Salt and freshly ground black pepper
1 small onion, quartered
200 g/7 oz/1 small can of pineapple cubes
½ green (bell) pepper, cut into cubes
Plain rice and a salad, to serve

1 Cut the meat into cubes and put into a small bowl. Add the oil, vinegar, salt and pepper. Stir so that all the meat is covered, and put aside to marinate for 1–2 hours.

2 When you are ready to cook, remove the meat from the marinade with a slotted spoon. Thread the meat on to skewers, alternating with the onion, pineapple and green pepper.

3 Cook under a hot grill (broiler), turning frequently, until the meat is browned on all sides.

4 Serve with rice and a salad.

🕐 10 minutes to prepare, plus marinating

Lamb with Courgettes and Mushrooms

15 ml/1 tbsp sunflower or vegetable oil
100 g/4 oz lamb fillet, thinly sliced
1 small onion, finely chopped
1 garlic clove, crushed
15 ml/1 tbsp tomato purée (paste)
300 ml/½ pint/1¼ cups hot chicken stock
5 ml/1 tsp chopped fresh rosemary
OR 2.5 ml/½ tsp dried rosemary
Salt and freshly ground black pepper
25 g/1 oz/2 tbsp butter or margarine
2 small courgettes (zucchini), sliced
50 g/2 oz button mushrooms
15 ml/1 tbsp plain yoghurt
Plain rice, to serve

1   Heat the oil in a frying pan (skillet) and fry (sauté) the lamb until well browned. Remove with a slotted spoon and drain on kitchen paper (paper towels).

2   Add the onion and garlic to the pan and fry (sauté) gently for about 5 minutes, until softened but not browned.

3   Stir the tomato purée into the hot stock, then pour into the pan. Add the meat, rosemary and salt and pepper to taste. Simmer, uncovered, for 20 minutes, or until the lamb is tender.

4   Melt the butter or margarine in a separate pan and toss the courgettes and mushrooms over a high heat for about 5 minutes.

5   Add the courgettes and mushrooms to the lamb, increase the heat and stir-fry until most of the liquid has evaporated and the sauce just coats the meat and vegetables.

6   Serve on a bed of rice, with the yoghurt spooned on top.

⏱ 35 minutes to prepare

Spicy Lamb Fillet

30 ml/2 tbsp plain Greek yoghurt
1 garlic clove, crushed
5 ml/1 tsp grated fresh root ginger
2.5 ml/½ tsp ground cumin
2.5 ml/½ tsp ground turmeric
10 ml/ 2 tsp lemon juice
Salt and freshly ground black pepper
100 g/4 oz lamb fillet
Warm pitta bread and a green salad, to serve

1   In a non-metallic bowl, mix together the yoghurt, garlic, ginger, cumin, turmeric and lemon juice. Season with salt and pepper.

2   Add the lamb fillet to the marinade, turn it to coat evenly and leave in a cool place for 2 hours.

3   Put the lamb under a hot grill (broiler) and cook for 3 minutes on each side, basting occasionally with the marinade.

4   Serve with warm pitta bread and a green salad.

⏱ 15 minutes to prepare, plus marinating

Ham Risotto

1 ham stock cube
120 ml/4 fl oz/½ cup boiling water
15 ml/1 tbsp sunflower or vegetable oil
1 small onion, sliced
½ green (bell) pepper, sliced
75 g/3 oz/¾ cup cooked ham, diced
50 g/2 oz/¼ cup Italian risotto (arborio) rice
1 tomato
Salt and freshly ground black pepper
25 g/1 oz/¼ cup Cheddar cheese, grated
A green salad, to serve

1   Dissolve the stock cube in the boiling water.

2   Heat the oil in a saucepan and fry (sauté) the onion and pepper until they are soft.

3   Add the ham to the saucepan. Fry gently for another 2 minutes. Add the rice and cook, stirring continuously, for another 2 minutes. Add the tomato and stir in the stock. Season with salt and pepper.

4   Bring to the boil and then reduce the heat until the liquid is simmering gently. Simmer for 12–15 minutes, until all the liquid is absorbed and the rice is tender.

5   Sprinkle with grated cheese, then serve with a green salad.

⏱ 20–25 minutes to prepare

✳ Ideally, a risotto should be made with round-grain Italian rice, but if you don't have any, you can use long-grain.

Ham Fried Rice

15 ml/1 tbsp sunflower or vegetable oil
1 egg, beaten
100 g/4 oz/½ cup cooked rice
Salt
50 g/2 oz/⅓ cup cooked ham, diced
90 g/3½ oz/1 small can of prawns (shrimp), drained
5 ml/1 tsp soy sauce
2–3 spring onions (scallions), chopped
2–3 lettuce leaves, shredded

1 Heat the oil in frying pan (skillet) or wok and pour in the beaten egg. When it is half set, mix in the cooked rice and add salt to taste.

2 Add the chopped ham and the prawns and continue to fry (sauté) for 5 minutes.

3 Sprinkle with soy sauce and mix in the chopped onions.

4 Arrange the shredded lettuce around a plate and spoon the rice mixture into the centre.

🕐 15 minutes to prepare

Pasta

Pasta is nutritious and healthy and makes perfect fast food for one, accompanied by nothing more complicated than a green salad. It may be bought fresh, which is quicker to cook and tastes better, or dried. The following are the more common types of pasta that you will find in your supermarket.

Spaghetti: Long, round, string-like pasta. Comes in various lengths and thicknesses. Vermicelli is thinner; capellini the thinnest.

Tagliatelli: Flat, ribbon noodles, made from egg pasta. Comes in strands or nests. There is also a green version.

Rigatoni: Short tubes with ridges.

Cannelloni: Large tubes for stuffing.

Ravioli: Squares with serrated edges, traditionally filled with spinach and Ricotta cheese, but often with meat.

Lasagne: Broad sheets of pasta for baking.

Shapes: Conchiglie (shells), farfalle (bows), fusilli (twists), and penne (tubes) all come in various sizes, and may be smooth or ridged.

Cooking Pasta

The method is the same whether you use fresh or dried pasta, but the time required will be different: fresh pasta takes about 3 minutes, dried about 12 minutes.

Bring to the boil a large saucepan of water. Add a pinch of salt and a few drops of olive oil, which will help stop the water boiling over. Put in the pasta. Long spaghetti or tagliatelli should be stood up in the saucepan and then pushed down as it softens. Let the water come to the boil again, then lower the heat and leave to simmer without a lid until the pasta is just cooked. The pasta should have a slight bite to it, which the Italians call *al dente*.

Pasta tastes delicious on its own. Stir 15 ml/1 tbsp of olive oil into the hot, cooked pasta and sprinkle on plenty of freshly ground black pepper. Alternatively, you can add one of the following to give extra flavour.

Parmesan cheese: Sprinkle over the hot, cooked pasta. You can buy ready-grated Parmesan in a drum, which is very convenient and keeps for ages in the fridge, but freshly grated Parmesan tastes much better.

Oil and garlic: For garlic-lovers only! Cook 6–8 cloves of chopped garlic in plenty of olive oil and pour over a dish of hot, cooked pasta. Add a good sprinkling of freshly ground black pepper, some chopped fresh parsley and 3–4 chopped anchovies, if liked.

Ready-made sauces: Most supermarkets now stock a wide range of sauces, such as Napoletana and Bolognese, in cans, cartons and jars to pour over your pasta.

Pesto: This is a strong, tangy sauce made from basil and pine nuts. Stir into the cooked pasta, and sprinkle Parmesan cheese on top, if liked.

Finally, it is quite simple to make your own fillings for cannelloni. Try any of the following mixtures.

Meat and herbs: 100 g/4 oz/1 cup finely chopped cooked meat, 1 beaten egg, some chopped fresh parsley, salt, pepper and grated nutmeg.

Two cheese: 100 g/4 oz/1 cup Ricotta cheese, 15 ml/1 tbsp grated Parmesan cheese,1 beaten egg and some chopped fresh parsley.

Spinach and Ricotta: 50 g/2 oz cooked spinach, 100 g/4 oz/ 1 cup Ricotta cheese, salt and pepper.

Spaghetti with Spicy Tomato Sauce

2 large ripe tomatoes
120 ml/4 fl oz/½ cup water
2.5 ml/½ tsp Worcestershire sauce
Salt and freshly ground black pepper
A pinch of garlic salt
75 g/3 oz spaghetti

1   Puncture the tomatoes and put them in boiling water until the skins split. Drop them into cold water, then remove the skins.

2   Chop the tomatoes and place in a small saucepan with the water, Worcestershire sauce, salt, pepper and garlic salt.

3   Simmer until the tomatoes are reduced to a smooth purée.

4   Meanwhile, bring a large pan of lightly salted water to the boil, add the spaghetti and cook for about 10 minutes, until tender. Drain through a sieve (strainer).

5   Spoon the tomato sauce over the cooked pasta.

 15 minutes to prepare

Spaghetti with Sunflower Seeds and Sun-dried Tomato

75 g/3 oz spaghetti
15 g/½ oz/1 tbsp sunflower seeds
15 g/½ oz/1 tbsp sun-dried tomato purée (paste)
1 garlic clove, crushed
Freshly ground black pepper
A little olive oil
15 ml/1 tbsp chopped fresh mixed herbs
15 ml/1 tbsp grated Parmesan cheese

1 Cook the spaghetti in boiling, salted water for about 10 minutes until just tender. Drain through a sieve (strainer).

2 Meanwhile, toast the sunflower seeds in a dry frying pan (skillet) until golden brown.

3 Allow the pan to cool slightly, then stir in the sun-dried tomato purée, garlic, pepper and a little olive oil (the amount you need depends on how thick the purée is). Stir over a medium heat for about 1 minute.

4 Stir the sauce and the herbs into the cooked spaghetti. Serve with Parmesan cheese sprinkled over the top.

 15 minutes to prepare

Fusilli with Smoked Haddock

50–75 g/2–3 oz fusilli
50–75 g/2–3 oz smoked haddock fillet
150 ml/¼ pint/⅔ cup milk
15 g/½ oz/1 tbsp butter or margarine
15 g/½ oz/2 tbsp plain (all-purpose) flour
1 hard-boiled (hard-cooked) egg, chopped
1 tomato, chopped
Salt and freshly ground black pepper
25 g/1 oz/¼ cup Cheddar cheese, grated

1 Cook the pasta in boiling, salted water according to the instructions on the packet.

2 Meanwhile, cook the fish in the milk for about 5 minutes. Pour off the milk into a jug. Remove the skin of the fish and flake the flesh.

3 Melt the butter or margarine in a saucepan, stir in the flour and cook for 1 minute. Remove the saucepan from the heat and stir in the reserved milk.

4 Return the saucepan to the heat and bring to the boil, stirring all the time to stop lumps forming. Turn down the heat and simmer gently for 2 minutes.

5 Add the flaked fish, the egg, tomato, salt, pepper and drained pasta. Mix well together and spoon into a flameproof dish.

6 Sprinkle the grated cheese on top and put under a hot grill (broiler) until golden brown.

 20 minutes to prepare

Linguine with Smoked Salmon and Mushrooms

15 ml/1 tbsp olive oil
50 g/2 oz button mushrooms, sliced
60 ml/4 tbsp dry white wine
2.5 ml/½ tsp chopped fresh dill
10 ml/2 tsp snipped fresh chives, plus extra for garnishing
120 ml/4 fl oz/½ cup fromage frais
50 g/2 oz smoked salmon
5 ml/1 tsp lemon juice
Salt and freshly ground black pepper
75 g/3 oz linguine

1 Heat the oil in a frying pan (skillet), add the mushrooms and cook over a gentle heat for 4–5 minutes, until softened.

2 Add the white wine, increase the heat and simmer for 5 minutes.

3 Stir in the herbs and fromage frais.

4 Cut the salmon into thin strips and add to the pan. Reheat gently, but do not allow to boil. Add the lemon juice and season with salt and pepper.

5 Meanwhile, cook the linguine in lightly salted, boiling water until just tender. Drain and turn on to a serving plate.

6 Spoon over the salmon sauce over the pasta and garnish with chives.

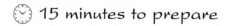 15 minutes to prepare

Pasta Shells with Ham and Cream Sauce

75 g/3 oz pasta shells
5 ml/2 tsp olive oil
2 spring onions (scallions), sliced
1 garlic clove, crushed
1 egg
30 ml/2 tbsp single (light) cream
15 ml/1 tbsp grated Parmesan cheese
Salt and freshly ground black pepper
50 g/2 oz/½ cup cooked ham, cut into strips

1 Cook the pasta in a large pan of boiling, salted water, according to the instructions on the packet.

2 Meanwhile, heat the oil in a small saucepan and fry (sauté) the onions and garlic for 3–4 minutes, until softened.

3 In a small bowl, beat together the egg, cream and Parmesan cheese. Season with salt and pepper.

4 Drain the pasta into a sieve (strainer), and then return it to the pan. Do not heat.

5 Immediately, add the beaten egg mixture, the cooked onion and garlic and ham. Toss thoroughly, then serve.

🕐 20 minutes to prepare

Penne in Tomato and Bacon Sauce

5 ml/2 tsp olive oil
1 small onion, sliced
A pinch of chilli powder
25–50 g/1–2 oz bacon, chopped
5 ml/1 tsp tomato purée (paste)
200 g/7 oz/1 small can of tomatoes
2.5 ml/½ tsp dried basil
Salt and freshly ground black pepper
75 g/3 oz penne
15 ml/1 tbsp grated Parmesan cheese

1   Heat the oil in a saucepan and fry (sauté) the onion gently for 4–5 minutes, until softened.

2   Add the chilli powder and chopped bacon, then cook for another 3–4 minutes.

3   Add the tomato purée, tomatoes and basil. Season with salt and pepper. Bring to the boil, then reduce the heat and simmer for 10–15 minutes.

4   Meanwhile, cook the pasta in a large pan of boiling, salted water, according to the instructions on the packet.

5   Drain the pasta well and add it to the hot sauce. Toss thoroughly.

6   Sprinkle with Parmesan cheese, then serve.

🕑 25 minutes to prepare

Tuna Pasta

75 g/3 oz pasta shapes
15 ml/1 tbsp olive oil
½ onion, sliced
½ red (bell) pepper, seeded and chopped
90 g/3½ oz/1 small can of tuna in brine
45 ml/3 tbsp canned or cooked frozen sweetcorn (corn)
5 ml/1 tsp lemon juice
15 ml/1 tbsp chopped fresh parsley

1 Cook the pasta in plenty of boiling, lightly salted water, according to the instructions on the packet. Drain into a sieve (strainer).

2 Meanwhile, heat the oil in a frying pan (skillet). Add the onion and pepper, and cook until softened but not browned.

3 Drain the tuna and add to the pan with the sweetcorn. Heat through.

4 Add the cooked pasta, lemon juice and parsley to the pan and heat through gently.

🕐 20 minutes to prepare

Farfalle with Goats' Cheese and Sesame Seeds

75 g/3 oz farfalle
5 ml/1 tsp sesame seeds
15 ml/1 tbsp olive oil
½ onion, chopped
30 ml/2 tbsp dry white wine
15 ml/1 tbsp vegetable or chicken stock
50 g/2 oz soft goats' cheese
Freshly ground black pepper
Grated Parmesan cheese, to garnish

1 Cook the farfalle in a large pan of boiling, salted water, according to the instructions on the packet.

2 Meanwhile, toast the sesame seeds in a dry frying pan (skillet).

3 Heat the oil and gently fry (sauté) the onion until softened but not browned.

4 Add the wine, stock and cheese. Stir gently until the cheese melts.

5 Season with black pepper and stir in the toasted sesame seeds.

6 Drain the cooked pasta and toss with the sauce, then sprinkle with grated Parmesan cheese.

🕐 15 minutes to prepare

Farfalle with Courgettes and Ham

75 g/3 oz farfalle
15 g/½ oz/1 tbsp butter or margarine
2 spring onions (scallions), finely chopped
25 g/1 oz button mushrooms, sliced
1 courgette (zucchini), thinly sliced
1 slice of ham, cut into strips
30 ml/2 tbsp crème fraîche
15 ml/1 tbsp grated Parmesan cheese
Freshly ground black pepper
Fresh basil leaves, to garnish

1 Cook the farfalle in a large pan of boiling, salted water, according to the instructions on the packet.

2 Meanwhile, melt the butter or margarine in a pan and cook the spring onions, mushrooms and courgette over a gentle heat for 6–8 minutes.

3 Stir in the ham, crème fraîche, Parmesan cheese and a good sprinkling of black pepper.

4 Drain the pasta and mix with the other ingredients in the pan. Heat through for a few moments, then spoon on to a warm plate.

5 Garnish with fresh basil.

 15 minutes to prepare

Pasta with Peperonata

5 ml/1 tsp olive oil
1 small onion, sliced
1 garlic clove, crushed
1 small red (bell) pepper, seeded and cut into strips
1 small yellow pepper, seeded and cut into strips
1 small green pepper, seeded and cut into strips
2 tomatoes, skinned and chopped
3–4 basil leaves, torn
A pinch of salt
75 g/3 oz pasta, any kind

1 Heat the oil and fry (sauté) the onion and garlic until lightly browned.

2 Add the peppers, cover and cook for 15 minutes.

3 Add the tomatoes, basil leaves and salt and cook for a further 10 minutes.

4 Meanwhile, cook the pasta in boiling, salted water, according to the instructions on the packet, then drain.

5 Spoon the peperonata over the pasta and serve.

🕐 30 minutes to prepare

Rigatoni with Peperoni Sausage

75 g/3 oz rigatoni
Salt and freshly ground black pepper
25 g/1 oz/2 tbsp butter or margarine
50 g/2 oz smoked sausage, thinly sliced
15 g/½ oz/2 tbsp plain (all-purpose) flour
120 ml/4 fl oz/½ cup milk
25 g/1 oz/¼ cup Gruyère (Swiss) cheese, grated
15 ml/1 tbsp tomato purée (paste)
4 slices of peperoni sausage
2 slices of Mozzarella cheese

1 Cook the rigatoni in a pan of boiling, salted water, according to the instructions on the packet. Drain, return to the saucepan and season well with salt and pepper. Add half the butter or margarine and the smoked sausage. Mix well and spoon into a flameproof dish.

2 Melt the remaining butter or margarine in a saucepan, stir in the flour and cook for 1 minute. Stir in the milk and bring the sauce to the boil, stirring, until it thickens.

3 Remove from the heat and stir in the grated cheese, then pour the cheese sauce over the rigatoni. Mix the tomato purée with 15 ml/1 tbsp hot water and pour over the top.

4 Arrange the slices of peperoni and Mozzarella on top and put under a hot grill (broiler) until the cheese is bubbling and golden brown.

⏱ 20 minutes to prepare

✖ If you don't have Gruyère cheese and Mozzarella, Cheddar will do almost as well.

Tagliatelli with Bacon and Mushrooms

75 g/3 oz tagliatelli
15 ml/1 tbsp sunflower or vegetable oil
50 g/2 oz mushrooms
1 garlic clove, crushed
2 rashers (slices) of smoked bacon, chopped
15 ml/1 tbsp white wine
1.5 ml/¼ tsp dried oregano
A small knob of butter or margarine
Freshly ground black pepper

1 Cook the tagliatelli in boiling, salted water, according to the instructions on the packet. Drain and set aside.

2 Meanwhile, heat the oil in a saucepan and gently fry (sauté) the mushrooms, garlic and bacon for 5 minutes.

3 Add the wine and continue cooking for another 5 minutes.

4 Stir in the cooked tagliatelli, the oregano and butter or margarine.

5 Season well with black pepper.

 15 minutes to prepare

Tagliatelli with Bacon and Pesto

75 g/3 oz tagliatelli
15 ml/1 tbsp olive oil
2 slices (rashers) of unsmoked bacon, chopped
1 garlic clove, crushed
15 ml/1 tbsp pesto
30 ml/2 tbsp crème fraîche
15 ml/1 tbsp grated Parmesan cheese
Freshly ground black pepper
6 black olives (optional)

1   Cook the tagliatelli in boiling, salted water, according to the instructions on the packet. Drain.

2   Meanwhile, heat the oil in a frying pan (skillet) and fry (sauté) the bacon and garlic for 5 minutes.

3   Add the drained tagliatelli, the pesto, crème fraîche and Parmesan cheese. Season with black pepper.

4   Spoon on to a warmed plate and arrange the olives on top, if liked.

 15 minutes to prepare

Tortellini with Mushroom Sauce

75 g/3 oz tortellini
15 g/½ oz/1 tbsp butter or margarine
2 spring onions (scallions), chopped
1 garlic clove, crushed
25 g/1 oz mushrooms, sliced
120 ml/4 fl oz/½ cup crème fraîche
15 ml/1 tbsp chopped fresh herbs, e.g. parsley, basil, oregano
Salt and freshly ground black pepper

1 Cook the tortellini for about 15 minutes, according to the instructions on the packet.

2 Meanwhile, melt the butter or margarine in a saucepan. Add the onions, garlic and mushrooms and cook gently for 5 minutes.

3 Add the crème fraîche and herbs and season with salt and pepper.

4 Drain the cooked tortellini and stir into the sauce.

🕑 15 minutes to prepare

✳ Tortellini are little parcels of stuffed pasta. You can buy them fresh or dried, filled with spinach and Ricotta, or beef and Mortadella. A packet of dried tortellini is a very useful item for the storecupboard, as it provides a quick and filling meal. Traditionally, tortellini are added to soups , but they are equally delicious as a main meal, served with Spicy Tomato Sauce (see page 99) or simply tossed in a little olive oil and sprinkled with grated Parmesan cheese.

Vegetarian Dishes

The recipes in this section, which are based on pulses and grains as well as vegetables, are so tasty that you will want to try them whether you are a vegetarian or not.

Pulses, such as lentils, chick peas (garbanzos) and beans, and grains, such as rice, bulgar (cracked wheat) and couscous, are an excellent replacement for meat because they contain valuable protein as well as important vitamins and minerals. They are also a rich source of complex carbohydrates and fibre, and contain no saturated fat.

Dried pulses are cheaper than the canned ones, but they require more effort because most of them need to be soaked for several hours and then cooked before they can be used. If you are eating on your own, it's much easier to open a small can.

Cauliflower, Potato and Pea Curry

45 ml/3 tbsp sunflower or vegetable oil
100 g/4 oz cauliflower florets
1 potato, peeled and cubed
1.5 ml/¼ tsp cumin seeds
1 green chilli, seeded and chopped
1.5 ml/¼ tsp grated fresh root ginger
2.5 ml/½ tsp ground cumin
2.5 ml/½ tsp ground turmeric
Salt and freshly ground black pepper
120 ml/4 fl oz/½ cup water
50 g/2 oz peas, shelled fresh or frozen
Naan bread, to serve

1 Heat the oil and fry (sauté) the cauliflower and potato until lightly browned.

2 Add the cumin seeds and fry for 1 minute.

3 Add the green chilli, ginger, cumin, turmeric, salt and pepper, stir well and fry for another minute.

4 Add the water and bring to the boil, then add the peas.

5 Cover and simmer for 10–15 minutes, until the cauliflower and potato are tender. Taste and adjust the seasoning.

6 Serve with warm naan bread.

🕐 25 minutes to prepare

Spinach and Potato Curry

75 g/3 oz frozen spinach
15 ml/1 tbsp sunflower or vegetable oil
2.5 ml/½ tsp black mustard seeds
½ onion, thinly sliced
1 garlic clove, crushed
5 ml/1 tsp grated fresh root ginger
200 g/7 oz potatoes, cubed
2.5 ml/½ tsp chilli powder
45 ml/3 tbsp water
Salt
Naan bread, to serve

1 Cook the spinach according to the packet instructions. Drain thoroughly, pressing down with a spoon to squeeze out all the liquid.

2 Heat the oil in a pan and fry (sauté) the mustard seeds for 2 minutes, or until they begin to splutter.

3 Add the onion, garlic and ginger and fry for 5 minutes, stirring.

4 Add the cubed potato, chilli powder, water and salt to taste. Cook for 8 minutes.

5 Add the drained spinach. Cover the pan with a tight-fitting lid and simmer for 10–15 minutes, until the potatoes are soft.

6 Serve with warm naan bread.

🕐 30 minutes to prepare

✱ This traditional Indian dish is dry, and quite spicy – reduce the amount of chilli powder if it is too hot for your taste.

Spicy Curried Mushrooms

15 ml/1 tbsp sunflower or vegetable oil
A knob of butter or margarine
1 potato, diced
1 small onion, chopped
1 garlic clove, crushed
2.5 ml/½ tsp grated fresh root ginger
2.5 ml/½ tsp ground cumin
2.5 ml/½ tsp ground coriander
2.5 ml/½ tsp ground turmeric
175 g/6 oz button mushrooms
2 tomatoes, skinned and chopped
15 ml/1 tbsp plain yoghurt
5 ml/1 tsp lemon juice
Salt and freshly ground black pepper
Brown rice, to serve

1 Heat the oil and butter or margarine in a saucepan and fry (sauté) the potato and onion for 4–5 minutes until softened.

2 Add the garlic, ginger and spices and cook for 1 minute.

3 Add the mushrooms, tomatoes, yoghurt and lemon juice. Season well with salt and pepper and cook for 20 minutes until thick.

4 Serve with brown rice.

🕐 30 minutes to prepare

.

Lentil Curry

15 ml/1 tbsp sunflower or vegetable oil
1 small onion, sliced
50 g/2 oz/⅓ cup red lentils
5 ml/1 tsp curry powder
15 ml/1 tbsp tomato purée (paste)
1 small potato, diced
1 carrot, diced
50 g/2 oz button mushrooms, sliced
50 g/2 oz peas, frozen or canned
Naan bread, to serve

1 Heat the oil in a saucepan and gently fry (sauté) the onion and lentils for 5 minutes.

2 Add just enough water to cover them and continue cooking for a further 10–15 minutes until the water is absorbed.

3 Add the curry powder and tomato purée, and stir well.

4 Add the vegetables and a little more water.

5 Cover and simmer for another 10–15 minutes, until the vegetables are cooked.

6 Serve with warm naan bread.

🕐 35 minutes to prepare

Spicy Chick Peas
with Tomato

200 g/7 oz/1 small can of chick peas (garbanzos)
15 ml/1 tbsp sunflower or vegetable oil
1 small onion, sliced
1 garlic clove, crushed
2.5 ml/½ tsp ground turmeric
2.5 ml/½ tsp paprika
2.5 ml/½ tsp ground cumin
2.5 ml/½ tsp ground coriander (cilantro)
2.5 ml/½ tsp garam masala
2 tomatoes, chopped
Salt and freshly ground black pepper
Brown rice or naan bread, to serve

1 Drain the chick peas through a sieve (strainer).

2 Heat the oil in a saucepan and fry (sauté) the onion and garlic for about 5 minutes, until softened.

3 Add the spices and continue cooking for another 2 minutes, stirring all the time.

4 Add the tomatoes and cook until they are soft.

5 Add the chick peas, stir well, and cook for another 5 minutes. Season with salt and pepper.

6 Serve with brown rice or naan bread.

⏱ **20 minutes to prepare**

Chick Pea and Pepper Stew

200 g/7 oz/1 small can of chick peas (garbanzos)
15 ml/1 tbsp sunflower or vegetable oil
1 small onion, sliced
1 garlic clove, crushed
½ green (bell) pepper, sliced
½ red pepper, sliced
Salt and freshly ground black pepper
30 ml/2 tbsp plain yoghurt
Brown rice or naan bread, to serve

1 Drain the chick peas through a sieve (strainer).

2 Heat the oil in a saucepan and gently fry (sauté) the onion and garlic for 2–3 minutes, until softened.

3 Add the peppers and cook for another 2–3 minutes.

4 Add the drained chick peas, and season with salt and pepper. Simmer gently for 10 minutes.

5 Stir in the yoghurt and continue cooking for 1–2 minutes until the stew has thickened.

6 Serve with brown rice or naan bread.

⏱ 20 minutes to prepare

Mexican Beans

200 g/7 oz/1 small can of red kidney beans
15 ml/1 tbsp sunflower or vegetable oil
1 small onion, thinly sliced
200 g/7 oz/1 small can of tomatoes
Salt and freshly ground black pepper
25 g/1 oz/¼ cup Cheddar cheese, grated (optional)
Plain rice, to serve

1 Drain the beans into a sieve (strainer) and rinse thoroughly under cold running water.

2 Heat the oil in a saucepan and fry (sauté) the onion gently for 5 minutes.

3 Add the tomatoes and continue cooking for another 5 minutes.

4 Add the drained beans. Season with salt and pepper. Simmer over a low heat for 20 minutes.

5 Stir in the cheese, if using. Serve with rice.

⊙ 30 minutes to prepare

✳ If you are a vegan, simply leave the cheese out.

Chilli Beans

200 g/7 oz/1 small can of red kidney beans
15 ml/1 tbsp sunflower or vegetable oil
1 small onion, sliced
1 small green or red (bell) pepper, sliced
2.5 ml/½ tsp chilli powder
2.5 ml/½ tsp dried mixed herbs
5 ml/1 tsp tomato purée (paste)
Salt and freshly ground black pepper
Plain rice, to serve

1   Drain the beans into a sieve (strainer) and rinse thoroughly under cold running water.

2   Heat the oil in a saucepan and gently fry (sauté) the onion and pepper for 5 minutes.

3   Add the beans and the rest of the ingredients and cook for another 10 minutes.

4   Serve with rice.

 15 minutes to prepare

Italian Bean Stew

200 g/7 oz/1 small can of cannellini or borlotti beans
15 ml/1 tbsp sunflower or vegetable oil
1 small onion, sliced
1 garlic clove, crushed
200 g/7 oz/1 small can of tomatoes
15 ml/1 tbsp tomato purée (paste)
50 g/2 oz pasta shapes
5 ml/1 tsp dried mixed herbs

1 Drain the beans through a sieve (strainer).

2 Heat the oil in a saucepan and fry (sauté) the onion and garlic for 2–3 minutes.

3 Add the beans, tomatoes and tomato purée and cook for another 2 minutes.

4 Add the pasta and dried herbs. Simmer gently for 7–8 minutes, until the pasta is cooked.

15 minutes to prepare

Cannellini Beans with Courgettes and Mushrooms

120 ml/4 fl oz/½ cup water
15 ml/1 tbsp tomato purée (paste)
15 ml/1 tbsp olive or sunflower oil
15 ml/1 tbsp wine vinegar
1 garlic clove, crushed
A pinch of ground coriander (cilantro)
Salt and freshly ground black pepper
1 small onion, chopped
1 small courgette (zucchini), sliced
50 g/2 oz button mushrooms, sliced
200 g/7 oz/1 small can of cannellini beans, drained
15 ml/1 tbsp chopped fresh parsley (optional)
Plain rice or pasta, to serve

1   Put the water, tomato purée, oil, vinegar, garlic, coriander, salt and pepper into a saucepan. Bring to the boil, then reduce the heat and simmer for 5 minutes.

2   Add the onion, courgette and mushrooms and cook for 3–5 minutes, until the vegetables are just cooked.

3   Add the drained beans and the parsley. Heat through for another minute and serve with rice or pasta.

⏱ 15 minutes to prepare

✳ This dish is also excellent cold. Eat half of it hot with rice or pasta, and keep the rest in the refrigerator overnight to eat the following day as a salad with French bread.

Bean Goulash

10 ml/2 tsp sunflower or vegetable oil
1 small onion, sliced
1 garlic clove, crushed (optional)
5–10 ml/1–2 tsp paprika
200 g/7 oz/1 small can of red kidney beans
200 g/7 oz/1 small can of borlotti or butter (lima) beans
200 g/7 oz/1 small can of tomatoes
Salt and freshly ground black pepper
Pitta bread, to serve

1 Heat the oil in a saucepan and fry (sauté) the onion and garlic for 3–4 minutes.

2 Add the paprika and cook for another minute.

3 Rinse and drain the beans and add to the pan with the tomatoes.

4 Simmer gently for 5 minutes until all the ingredients are heated through.

5 Season to taste.

6 Serve with pitta bread.

⏱ 10 minutes to prepare

✳ This simple goulash can be made with whatever cans of beans you have in your storecupboard. Eaten with pitta bread, this is a quick, nourishing and filling meal for a cold day. If there is too much for one meal, it can be reheated and will taste even better.

Tunisian Aubergine

1 aubergine (eggplant)
Salt
15 ml/1 tbsp olive oil
½ onion, sliced
1 garlic clove, crushed
A pinch of cayenne
2.5 ml/½ tsp ground cumin
2.5 ml/½ tsp ground coriander (cilantro)
2–3 tomatoes, chopped
15 ml/1 tbsp raisins
10 ml/2 tsp chopped fresh mint
OR 5 ml/1 tsp dried mint
Freshly ground black pepper
Brown rice, to serve

1 Cut the aubergine into 1 cm/½ in cubes and put into a colander. Sprinkle with salt and leave for 15 minutes.

2 Heat the oil, add the onion and garlic and fry (sauté) gently until softened. Stir in the cayenne, cumin and coriander and cook for 2 minutes.

3 Rinse the aubergine cubes and pat dry with kitchen paper (paper towels). Add to the pan and cook until browned.

4 Stir in the tomatoes, raisins and mint, and add black pepper to taste. Cook gently until almost all the liquid has evaporated and the aubergine is tender.

5 Serve with brown rice.

🕐 *30 minutes to prepare*

Persian Aubergine with Bulgar

1 small aubergine (eggplant)
Salt
50 g/2 oz/½ cup bulgar (cracked wheat)
250 ml/8 fl oz/1 cup water
30 ml/2 tbsp olive oil
1 small onion, sliced
5 ml/1 tsp ground cumin
5 ml/1 tsp ground coriander (cilantro)
25 g/1 oz/3 tbsp raisins
25 g/1 oz/2 tbsp flaked (slivered) almonds
Freshly ground black pepper

1   Chop the aubergine into small cubes. Sprinkle with salt and leave for 15 minutes.

2   Put the bulgar and water into a saucepan, bring to the boil, then reduce the heat and simmer for 10 minutes until all the water has been absorbed.

3   Meanwhile, heat the oil and cook the onion until softened.

4   Add the aubergine and stir-fry until lightly brown.

5   Add the cumin, coriander, raisins and almonds and cook for 1 minute.

6   Stir in the bulgar and season with plenty of pepper.

🕐 20 minutes to prepare

Bulgar with Avocado and Toasted Seeds

50 g/2 oz/½ cup bulgar (cracked wheat)
250 ml/8 fl oz/1 cup water
10 ml/2 tsp sesame seeds
10 ml/2 tsp sunflower seeds
1 small avocado, peeled and chopped
2 spring onions (scallions)
2.5 cm/1 in piece of cucumber, diced
25 g/1 oz/3 tbsp raisins
15 g/½ oz/1 tbsp walnuts, chopped
15 ml/1 tbsp chopped fresh coriander (cilantro)
10 ml/2 tsp lemon juice
15 ml/1 tbsp olive oil
Salt and fresh ground black pepper

1　Put the bulgar and water into a saucepan, bring to the boil, then reduce the heat and simmer for 10 minutes, until all the water has been absorbed. Turn into a bowl.

2　Meanwhile, toast the sesame and sunflower seeds in a hot dry frying pan (skillet).

3　Stir half the avocado, the spring onions, cucumber, raisins, walnuts, coriander and toasted seeds into the bulgar.

4　Mix together the lemon juice and olive oil. Season with salt and pepper and pour over the bulgar mixture. Toss well and garnish with the remaining avocado.

🕐 15 minutes to prepare

Vegetable Pilau

100 g/4 oz/½ cup basmati rice
15 ml/1 tbsp sunflower or vegetable oil
2.5 ml/½ tsp cumin seeds
1 bay leaf
3 green cardamom pods
3 whole cloves
½ onion, finely chopped
1 small carrot, finely chopped
25 g/1 oz peas, thawed if frozen
25 g/1 oz sweetcorn (corn), thawed if frozen
25 g/1 oz/¼ cup cashew nuts
250 ml/8 fl oz/1 cup water
1.5 ml/¼ tsp ground coriander (cilantro)
1.5 ml/¼ tsp ground cumin
Salt
Sprigs of coriander, to garnish

1 Put the rice in a sieve (strainer) and wash thoroughly under cold running water. Leave to drain.

2 Heat the oil in a large pan and fry (sauté) the cumin seeds for 2 minutes. Add the bay leaf, cardamoms and cloves and fry for 2 minutes. Add the onion and fry for 5 minutes, until lightly browned.

3 Stir in the carrot and cook for 3 minutes. Add the rice, peas, sweetcorn and cashew nuts. Fry for 5 minutes.

4 Pour in the water, then add the ground spices and salt to taste. Bring to the boil.

5 Leave to stand for 5–10 minutes, then garnish with coriander sprigs and serve.

🕐 30 minutes to prepare

Spicy Mexican Rice

15 g/½ oz/1 tbsp butter or margarine
100 g/4 oz/½ cup long-grain rice
200 g/7 oz/1 small can of tomatoes
150 ml/¼ pt/⅔ cup vegetable stock
2.5 ml/½ tsp chilli powder
Salt and freshly ground black pepper
1 red (bell) pepper, sliced into rings
1 onion, sliced into rings

1   Melt the butter or margarine in a pan, add the rice and fry (sauté) gently for 2–3 minutes.

2   Add the tomatoes, stock and chilli powder, and season with salt and pepper. Bring to the boil and stir.

3   Lay the pepper and onion rings on top of the rice. Cover the pan with a lid, turn down the heat and simmer for 15 minutes, until all the liquid has been absorbed and the rice is tender.

🕐 25 minutes to prepare

✶   This spicy dish is quite hot – adjust the amount of chilli powder to suit your taste.

Spinach and Mushroom Risotto

10 ml/2 tsp olive oil
1 small onion, finely chopped
50 g/2 oz/¼ cup Italian risotto (arborio) rice
300 ml/10 fl oz/1¼ cups vegetable stock
100 g/4 oz mushrooms, chopped
75 g/3 oz spinach, fresh or frozen
5 ml/1 tsp lemon juice
Salt and freshly ground black pepper
A pinch of grated nutmeg
15 ml/1 tbsp grated Parmesan cheese (optional)

1 Heat the oil in a saucepan and add the chopped onion. Cook gently until the onion is softened.

2 Stir in the rice, and after cooking for 1 minute add the stock. Bring to the boil, then reduce the heat and simmer for about 10 minutes, until almost all the stock has been absorbed.

3 Add the mushrooms, spinach and lemon juice. Cook for a further 2–3 minutes, stirring occasionally.

4 Season with salt, pepper and nutmeg.

5 Sprinkle with Parmesan cheese, if liked, then serve

⏱ 30–35 minutes to prepare

✱ You can use long-grain rice but round-grain risotto rice gives a much better result.

Couscous with Mushrooms

100 g/4 oz/1 cup quick-cook couscous
150 ml/¼ pint/⅔ cup boiling water
Grated rind and juice of ½ lemon
Salt and freshly ground black pepper
40 g/1½ oz/3 tbsp butter or margarine
100 g/4 oz mushrooms, sliced
5 ml/1 tsp Dijon mustard
15 g/½ oz/1 tbsp pine nuts
Sprigs of parsley, to garnish

1   Put the couscous in a bowl and pour over the boiling water. Add the lemon rind and season with salt and pepper. Leave to soak for 5–10 minutes, stirring occasionally.

2   Meanwhile, melt half the butter or margarine in a frying pan (skillet). Add the mushrooms and fry (sauté) gently until softened. Remove from the heat and stir in the mustard and 5 ml/1 tsp lemon juice.

3   Melt the remaining butter or margarine in a separate pan. Add the pine nuts and couscous and cook over a high heat, stirring, until piping hot. Season with salt and pepper.

4   Spoon the couscous mixture on to a warm plate and pile the mushrooms on top. Garnish with fresh parsley sprigs.

 10 minutes to prepare

Salads

The salads described in this section are complete meals in themselves if eaten with some good, crusty bread, and they make an ideal summer lunch or supper. Leftover cooked pasta, rice or potatoes can always be used as part of a salad, so it's a good idea occasionally to cook a little extra, ready for the next meal.

Making your own French dressing is very simple: just put 30 ml/2 tbsp olive oil, 15 ml/ 1 tbsp wine vinegar, 5 ml/1 tsp sugar, 5 ml/ 1 tsp mustard powder and some salt and freshly ground black pepper into a screwtop jar and shake well before using.

Greek Salad

3–4 lettuce leaves
2 ripe tomatoes
½ small sweet cucumber
6 black olives
50 g/2 oz/½ cup Feta cheese, cubed
15 ml/1 tbsp olive oil
10 ml/2 tsp wine vinegar or lemon juice
10 ml/2 tsp chopped fresh herbs
Salt and freshly ground black pepper

1   Wash the lettuce leaves, tear or shred them and arrange on a plate.

2   Chop the tomatoes and cucumber and arrange on top of the lettuce.

3   Add the olives and cubes of Feta cheese.

4   Mix the oil, vinegar or lemon juice, herbs and seasoning together and pour over the salad.

⏱ 5 minutes to prepare

✖ Anyone who has been on holiday to Greece will have eaten this traditional salad, served in tavernas as a light lunch or as a starter to a main meal. Vary the quantities of the different ingredients according to your personal preference.

Swiss Salad

50 g/2 oz/½ cup Gruyère (Swiss) cheese, cubed
1 slice of cooked ham, chopped
2–3 cooked potatoes, diced
2–3 lettuce leaves
30 ml/2 tbsp plain yoghurt
2.5 ml/½ tsp made mustard
5 ml/½ tsp lemon juice
Salt and freshly ground black pepper
1 egg, hardboiled (hard-cooked)

1 Place the cheese, ham and potato in a bowl.

2 Shred the lettuce leaves finely and add to the bowl.

3 In another bowl, mix together the yoghurt, mustard, lemon juice and a little salt and pepper. Pour over the salad and toss lightly.

4 Cut the egg into wedges and arrange on top of the salad.

⏱ 5 minutes to prepare

Salade Niçoise

100 g/4 oz French (green) beans
15 ml/1 tbsp olive oil
10 ml/2 tsp wine vinegar
Salt and freshly ground black pepper
3 lettuce leaves
1 egg, hard-boiled (hard-cooked)
2 spring onions (scallions), chopped
1 tomato, quartered
90 g/3½ oz/1 small can of tuna fish
2 anchovies, drained and chopped (optional)
½ small green (bell) pepper, chopped
6 black olives

1   Cut the beans in half (leave them whole if they are small) and cook in boiling, salted water for 5–7 minutes, until just tender. Drain into a colander and rinse under cold, running water.

2   Mix the beans with the oil, vinegar, salt and pepper and arrange on a plate.

3   Wash the lettuce leaves and arrange on top of the beans.

4   Shell and halve the hard-boiled egg and arrange on top of the lettuce with the spring onions and tomato.

5   Turn the tuna fish into the centre.

6   Scatter the chopped anchovy fillets round the salad with the pepper and olives.

🕐 10 minutes to prepare

Pasta, Bacon and Bean Salad

50 g/2 oz streaky bacon, chopped
10 ml/2 tsp olive oil
2.5 ml/½ tsp made mustard
5 ml/1 tsp wine vinegar
2.5 ml/½ tsp clear honey
Salt and freshly ground black pepper
75 g/3 oz cooked fusilli
50 g/2 oz cooked French (green) beans, chopped
10 ml/2 tsp snipped fresh chives

1   Cook the chopped bacon in a dry frying pan (skillet) until it is crisp.

2   Remove from the heat and add the oil, mustard, vinegar and honey. Mix well and season to taste.

3   Add the cooked pasta and beans, and toss until everything is well mixed.

4   Sprinkle with chives.

5 minutes to prepare

Lobio

200 g/7 oz/1 small can of red kidney beans
1 garlic clove, crushed
1 small onion, finely chopped
1 tomato, chopped
15 ml/1 tbsp chopped fresh mixed herbs
OR 5 ml/1 tsp dried mixed herbs
15 ml/1 tbsp wine vinegar
15 ml/1 tbsp olive oil
Salt and freshly ground black pepper
50 g/2 oz/½ cup Feta cheese, crumbled

1   Mix together the beans, garlic, onion, tomato and herbs.

2   Pour over the vinegar and oil.

3   Season with salt and pepper and toss gently.

4   Sprinkle the Feta cheese over the top.

🕐 5 minutes to prepare

✳ This bean salad is a Russian dish.

Tuna and Butter Bean Salad

3–4 lettuce leaves
90 g/3½ oz/1 small can of tuna fish
200 g/7 oz/1 small can of butter (lima) beans
15 ml/1 tbsp French dressing (see page 132)

1 Wash the lettuce leaves and arrange them on a plate.

2 Drain and flake the tuna fish.

3 Drain the beans into a sieve (strainer) and rinse well under cold running water.

4 Mix the tuna fish and beans in a bowl with the French dressing and spoon on to the lettuce leaves.

🕑 5 minutes to prepare

Rice and Chicken Salad

75 g/3 oz/¾ cup cooked rice
15 ml/1 tbsp olive oil
15 ml/1 tbsp wine vinegar
Salt and freshly ground black pepper
75 g/3 oz/¾ cup cooked chicken, chopped
50 g/2 oz button mushrooms, sliced
½ green (bell) pepper, chopped
1 tomato, sliced

1 Place the rice in a bowl. Add the oil, vinegar, salt and pepper and mix thoroughly.

2 Just before you are ready to eat, add the chicken and vegetables.

🕐 5 minutes to prepare

✶ When you are cooking rice to serve with a meal, cook an extra portion to make this salad dish. Mix the rice while still warm with the oil and vinegar, so that it absorbs the flavours, then chill until required. Some chopped ham or tuna fish could be substituted for the chicken, and you could add other ingredients, such as sweetcorn (corn), beansprouts or cooked peas.

Chicken, Fruit and Pasta Salad

5 ml/1 tsp olive oil
75 g/3 oz cooked pasta shells
1 small eating (dessert) apple, diced
1 banana, sliced
10 ml/2 tsp lemon juice
75 g/3 oz/¾ cup cooked chicken, cubed
15 g/½ oz/1 tbsp walnuts, chopped
15 ml/1 tbsp mayonnaise

1   Stir the olive oil into the cooked pasta.

2   Put the apple and banana in a small bowl and sprinkle with the lemon juice.

3   Add the fruit to the pasta, with the chicken and walnuts.

4   Stir in the mayonnaise.

5   Chill in the refrigerator before serving.

🕐 5 minutes to prepare, plus chilling

Salami, Bean and Pasta Salad

50 g/2 oz cooked penne
50 g/2 oz salami, chopped
50 g/2 oz canned or cooked dried red kidney beans
2 spring onions (scallions), chopped
30 ml/2 tbsp plain yoghurt
5 ml/1 tsp made mustard
Lettuce leaves, to serve

1 Put the cooked penne into a bowl with the salami, beans and
spring onions.

2 Mix the yoghurt and mustard together and stir into the salad
ingredients.

3 Serve on a bed of lettuce.

⏱ 5 minutes to prepare

Ciabatta Salad

Ciabatta bread
2 plum tomatoes, cut into chunks
5 cm/2 in piece of cucumber, cut into chunks
½ small red onion, sliced
6 black olives
15 ml/1 tbsp chopped fresh parsley
15 ml/1 tbsp French dressing (see page 132)

1   Break the ciabatta into bite-sized pieces. Grill (broil) the bread for 2–3 minutes, until golden all over.

2   Mix the grilled bread with all the remaining ingredients. Leave to stand for 30 minutes before serving to allow the flavours to develop.

🕐 5 minutes to prepare, plus standing

✶ Use as much ciabatta bread as you like!

Noodle Salad

75 g/3 oz medium egg noodles
5 ml/1 tsp sesame seeds
1 carrot, grated
50 g/2 oz beansprouts
25 g/1 oz baby spinach leaves, rocket or crisp lettuce, shredded
2–3 spring onions (scallions), thinly sliced
5 ml/1 tsp finely chopped fresh coriander (cilantro) or parsley
5 ml/1 tsp chilli sauce
5 ml/1 tsp sesame oil
15 ml/1 tbsp soy sauce

1 Put the noodles into a large pan of boiling water. Bring back to the boil, reduce the heat and simmer for 4 minutes. Drain, rinse in cold water and put into a bowl.

2 Heat a small frying pan (skillet) and toast the sesame seeds for 2 minutes.

3 Add the vegetables and herbs to the noodles, toss well and sprinkle with toasted sesame seeds.

10 minutes to prepare

Desserts

Eating some fresh fruit is the quickest and easiest way to finish your meal but for a special treat, here are a few quick and easy desserts.

Honey Nut Banana

1 banana
15 g/½ oz/1 tbsp butter or margarine
15 ml/1 tbsp clear honey or syrup
15 ml/1 tbsp chopped nuts

1   Peel the banana and cut in half lengthways.

2   Melt the butter or margarine in a frying pan (skillet) and gently fry (sauté) the banana until soft.

3   Lift out on to a warm plate. Spoon over the honey or syrup and top with chopped nuts.

🕐 5–10 minutes to prepare

✖ Peaches, nectarines and plums are equally nice cooked in this way.

Pancakes

Makes 6–8 pancakes
100 g/4 oz/1 cup plain (all-purpose) flour
A pinch of salt
1 egg
300 ml/½ pt/1¼ cups milk
Sunflower or vegetable oil or lard (shortening), for cooking

1   Sift the flour and salt into a mixing bowl, make a well in the centre and break the egg into it. Using a wooden spoon, stir the egg and draw in the flour from around the sides.

2   Gradually add just enough milk to incorporate all the flour and make a thick paste. Beat very well to remove all the lumps so that the mixture is smooth.

3   Stir in the remaining milk, a little at a time. Beat the batter thoroughly until small air bubbles appear all over the surface. Leave the batter to stand for up to 1 hour, if you have time.

4   When you are ready to make the pancakes, heat a frying pan (skillet) until it is really hot. Put in 5 ml/½ tsp oil or a small knob of lard and allow this to spread all around the pan.

5   Pour in a little batter and tilt the pan so that it covers the base in a very thin layer.

6   Cook for about 1 minute, shaking the pan a little to stop it sticking, until the top is just set and the underneath is lightly browned, then turn the pancake over and cook for about another 20 seconds until the other side is browned.

   ⏱ 10 minutes to prepare, plus standing

* Once you have made the pancakes, they can be stored for a week in the fridge (or they can be frozen), so it is a good idea to make more than you need for one meal.

* To reheat the pancakes that you have stored in the fridge, put them between two plates on top of a pan of simmering water; or warm them under the grill (broiler).

Apple Fritters

1 quantity of pancake batter (see page 146), made with half the quantity of milk
A little sunflower or vegetable oil, for cooking
1 cooking (tart) apple, peeled, cored and sliced into rings
Sugar, for sprinkling

1 Make the batter – it will be thicker than pancake batter, as you are using less milk.

2 Pour oil into a frying pan (skillet) to a depth of about 1 cm/ ½ in and heat until a faint smoke is rising from it.

3 Dip the pieces of apple in the batter so that they are thickly coated, and then lower them into the hot oil.

4 Cook the fritters until they are a deep golden brown, then lift out with a slotted spoon and drain on kitchen paper (paper towels).

5 Sprinkle with sugar while still hot.

🕐 15 minutes to prepare

* You can make these with a banana, cut into four pieces, or drained, canned pineapple rings, if you prefer.

147

Banana Smoothie

1 banana
150 ml/¼ pt/⅔ cup plain yoghurt
15 ml/1 tbsp clear honey
150 ml/¼ pt/⅔ cup cold milk

1   Peel and roughly chop the banana.

2   Put all the ingredients into a food processor or blender and blend until smooth.

3   Serve in a tall glass.

🕐 2 minutes to prepare

✳ You will need a food processor or blender for this delicious dessert, which is equally good for breakfast. Try it with other soft fruit, such as strawberries.

Coffee Banana Dessert

5 ml/1 tsp coffee powder
5 ml/1 tsp boiling water
150 ml/¼ pt/⅔ cup plain yoghurt
Sugar, to taste
1 ripe banana, sliced

1 In a bowl, dissolve the coffee powder in the boiling water.

2 Beat in the yoghurt, and add sugar to taste.

3 Reserving few slices of banana for decoration, roughly mash the remainder and stir into the yoghurt.

4 Spoon into a serving dish and decorate with the reserved slices of banana.

🕐 5 minutes to prepare

Chocolate Pudding

Makes 2 servings

25 g/1 oz/¼ cup cornflour (cornstarch)
25 g/1 oz/¼ cup cocoa (unsweetened chocolate) powder
25 g/1 oz/2 tbsp caster (superfine) sugar
300 ml/½ pt/1¼ cups milk
Single (light) cream, to serve

1 Put the cornflour, cocoa powder and sugar into a small bowl and stir in enough milk to make a thinnish paste. Make sure the ingredients are really well mixed and there are no lumps of cornflour.

2 Pour the remaining milk into a small saucepan and heat until almost boiling.

3 Stir the hot milk into the chocolate mixture.

4 Mix well, then pour the whole lot back into the saucepan and cook on a moderate heat, stirring continuously, until the mixture is boiling and has thickened.

5 Remove from the heat and pour back into the basin. Sprinkle a little sugar on top to prevent a skin forming.

6 Serve warm or cold, with a little cream.

🕐 10 minutes to prepare

✳ This is almost as quick and easy to make as the synthetic whips that you buy in a packet and it tastes much better. Eat half of it warm, with a little cream, and the second helping will keep in the fridge to eat cold the following day.

Summer Pudding

Makes 2 servings

450 g/1 lb soft fruit, such as raspberries, blackberries
or redcurrants
Caster (superfine) sugar, to taste
4–5 thin slices of bread

1 Taste the fruit and add sugar if necessary.

2 Cut the crusts off the bread and use about three-quarters to line a bowl, fitting the slices closely together.

3 Put in the fruit, then lay the remainder of the bread on top so that the fruit is completely covered.

4 Put a plate with a weight on it on top of the pudding and chill for 24 hours. The fruit juice should have soaked through all the bread.

5 Turn out on to a serving plate.

⏲ 10 minutes to prepare, plus chilling

✸ This is a handy way of using up old bread and you can use stewed, canned, bottled or frozen fruit.

Fresh Fruit Salad

225 g/8 oz mixed fresh fruit ·
300 ml/½ pt/1¼ cups water
50 g/2 oz/¼ cup sugar
15 ml/1 tbsp lemon juice
Single (light) cream, to serve (optional)

1 Prepare the fruit (see note below).

2 Put the water and sugar into a small saucepan and boil for 5 minutes. Add the lemon juice.

3 Put the prepared fruit into a dish and pour over the syrup. Cover the bowl and leave to cool completely.

4 Serve with cream, if liked.

⏲ 5 minutes to prepare, plus cooling

✳ Use whatever fresh fruit you have available: apples, oranges, pears, seedless grapes, melon, raspberries and strawberries are all delicious and of course nowadays there is a wonderful selection of more exotic fruit available, such as kiwi fruit, mango and starfruit. Peel, core and chop all the fruit, as appropriate, before you make the syrup, except for banana, which should be added just before serving, otherwise it goes brown.

Crunchy Fruit Yoghurt Fool

1 peach
3–4 strawberries
150 ml/¼ pt/⅔ cup plain or strawberry yoghurt
10 ml/2 tsp porridge oats
10 ml/2 tsp flaked (slivered) almonds

1 Cut the peach in half, remove the stone (pit) and cut the flesh into slices. Hull the strawberries and halve or quarter them, depending on size.

2 Put the fruit into a serving bowl and stir in the yoghurt.

3 Toast the porridge oats and almonds in a hot, dry frying pan (skillet), until lightly browned. Cool, then sprinkle over the fruit and yoghurt.

🕐 5–10 minutes to prepare

✖ This works equally well with other soft fruits, such as nectarines, raspberries, apricots, kiwi fruit, pears, bananas or fresh or canned pineapple chunks. Just choose a flavoured yoghurt to match.

Spicy Nectarine

1 nectarine, halved and stoned (pitted)
100 ml/3½ fl oz/scant ½ cup apple juice
A pinch of ground cinnamon
A pinch of grated nutmeg
1 whole clove
25 g/1 oz/¼ cup bulgar (cracked wheat)

1 Put all the ingredients into a pan and bring to the boil. Reduce the heat and simmer gently for about 10 minutes, until the fruit is soft.

2 Remove the clove, then serve hot or cold.

⏱ 10 minutes to prepare

✳ Peaches, plums or pears work equally well in this recipe. The bulgar helps to thicken the sauce.

Instant Fruit Cheesecake

2 digestive biscuits (graham crackers)
50 g/2 oz/¼ cup cream cheese
30 ml/2 tbsp fromage frais
Caster (superfine) sugar, to taste
2 strawberries
5–6 raspberries

1 Crumble the biscuits (cookies) into a small dessert bowl and crush the crumbs with the bowl of a spoon.

2 Beat together the cream cheese and fromage frais, with a little sugar to taste. Spoon over the biscuit crumbs.

3 Top with the strawberries and raspberries.

🕑 5 minutes to prepare

✴ Not quite the real thing but it tastes just as good and is made in an instant. Use any kind of fresh fruit.

Peach in Brandy

1 peach
45 ml/3 tbsp water
25 g/1 oz/2 tbsp caster (superfine) sugar
15 ml/1 tbsp brandy
Single (light) cream, to serve

1   Skin, stone (pit) and halve the peach.

2   Put the water and sugar in a small pan and stir over a low heat to dissolve the sugar. Bring up to the boil, remove from the heat and add the peach halves.

3   Replace over a low heat, cover and simmer for about 5 minutes, until the peach is soft.

4   Lift the peach into a serving dish. Stir the brandy into the juice and pour over the peach.

5   Serve with cream.

10 minutes to prepare

✸ For that indulgent night in, treat yourself with this luxurious dessert. Make it ahead of time and leave it in the fridge to chill.

Index